Walk!

A Celebration of Striding Out

Colin Speakman

GREAT NORTHERN

Great Northern Books
PO Box 213, Ilkley, LS29 9WS
www.greatnorthernbooks.co.uk

ISBN: 978 1 905080 861

Design and layout: David Burrill

CIP Data
A catalogue for this book is available from the British Library

Colin Speakman is one of the founding members of the Yorkshire Dales Society. He is a keen walker and is credited with creating the popular Dales Way route, which runs from Ilkley to Windermere. He has written over 40 books and is a proactive campaigner for better public transport in rural areas, helping to set up the successful DalesBus Network.

Published in association with the
Campaign for National Parks
(registered charity number 295336)

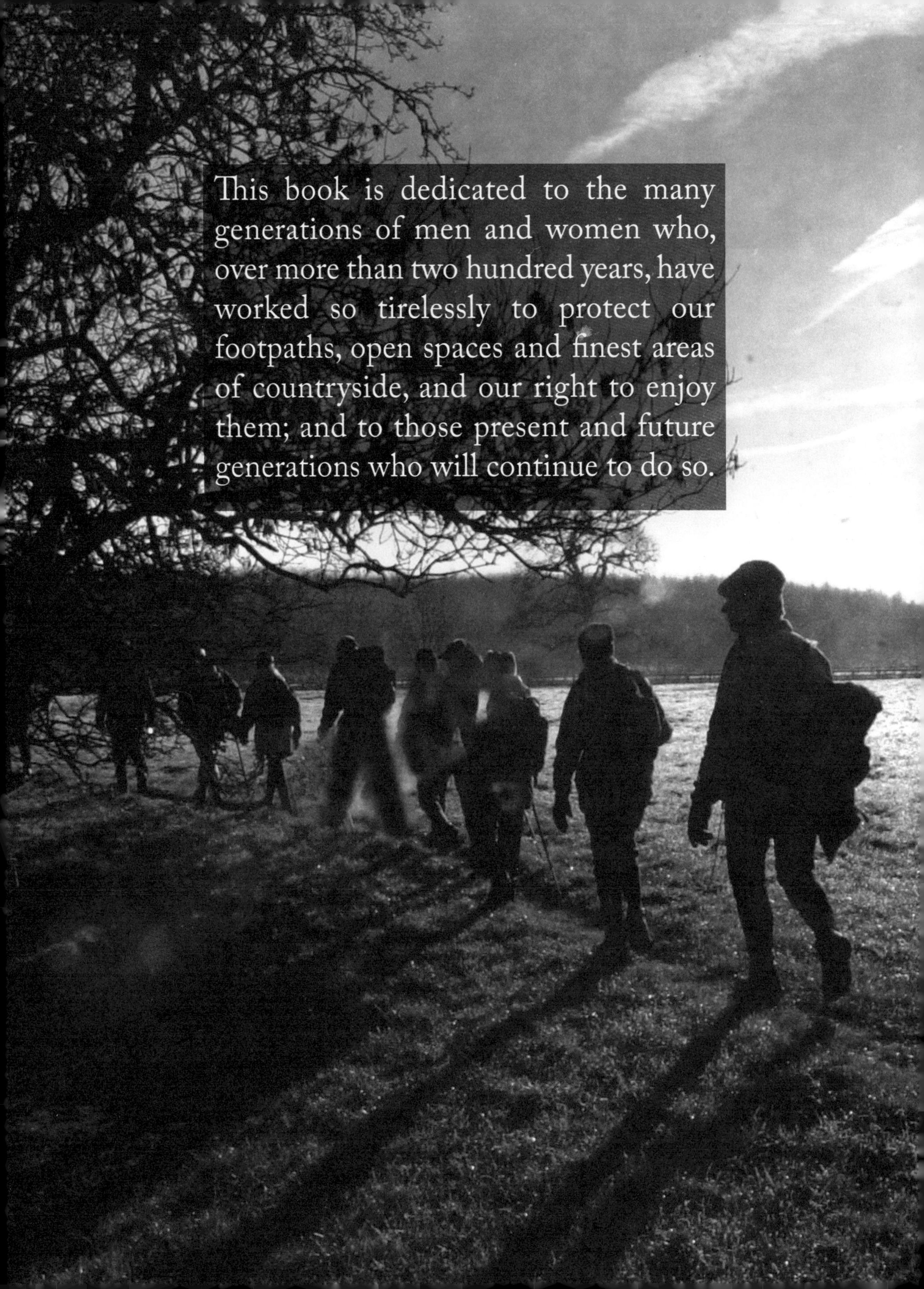

This book is dedicated to the many generations of men and women who, over more than two hundred years, have worked so tirelessly to protect our footpaths, open spaces and finest areas of countryside, and our right to enjoy them; and to those present and future generations who will continue to do so.

CONTENTS

"Colin Speakman's 'Walk!' should encourage many more people to walk in Britain's magnificent green spaces. Walking brings moments of inspiration, moments of calm, moments of serenity and most of all some good old exercise and fresh air. So get out there and get closer to nature - it's the simplest medicine in the world."

Dame Fiona Reynolds,
Director-General, The National Trust

Front cover and page 1: R Bryant collection
Back cover (top) and page 6: Anne Purkiss, South Downs Joint Committee
Back cover (bottom): Chris Bonington Picture Library. www.bonington.com
Pages 2-3 and 4-5: Yorkshire Post Newspapers

Foreword – 1

by BEN FOGLE

There are thousands of books on walks but nothing like this one. It skilfully traces the evolution of walking from the earliest days of exploring wild places. It looks in depth at the great campaigns for access to once forbidden land, with the resulting creation of National Parks and long-distance trails. It must surely be the first time the whole story has been brought together in one place.

Yet this is not just a book about the past or even the present. It looks to the future and makes fundamental points that accord with my own beliefs.

I spent most of my childhood roaming the South Downs and found it a glorious experience. It inspired me to pursue the adventures I now enjoy as an adult. I'm delighted that my current role as President of the Campaign for National Parks has coincided with the designation of the South Downs as a National Park. During a celebratory walk, I stressed that the key to the future of such unique areas was accessibility, so as to "ensure that everyone regardless of age or ability can have access to these wonderful landscapes". I also applauded schemes to encourage people of ethnic diversity as well as younger generations to enjoy and care about our National Parks: "Without them, their very future will be in jeopardy. We can protect their future best by getting out and enjoying and using them."

It is the means of "getting out" that forms some of the most thought-provoking sections of this book. Many will surely support the author's plea for walking to be re-invented as a key lifestyle choice to escape from car dependency. He sees such a move as heralding an inevitable return to less energy-profligate ways of travelling, which realistically would include not just walking but also cycling and using local buses and trains.

Not everyone will share such views, especially at a time when surveys have shown that an increasing number of young people feel terrified of going out into the countryside and prefer to remain indoors glued to their computer screens. Yet it is clear the situation is changing for reasons that were not anticipated. Ironically, it has taken a recession and an era of increasing stress to highlight the fact that there is nothing better than a good walk to improve health and happiness.

Media advice on how to survive the downturn now invariably includes taking a walk, as it costs nothing, can fit into a daily schedule, and saves money spent on petrol. It is also an attractive alternative to health club fees costing many hundreds of pounds a year. Medical experts have long insisted that a third of deaths caused by heart disease are related to inactivity and that walking improves both energy levels and sleeping patterns. Their views are at last being taken seriously.

This outstanding book could not therefore be more timely. It has been written when England and Wales still boast one of the best-maintained footpath networks in the world. Those who have cared for it are now falling easy prey to local government cuts with sad consequences. I cannot help thinking that a tiny fraction of the untold millions spent by the NHS on treating obesity might be better devoted to keeping paths in good order.

Have a good read, but do remember to take a break every so often rather than just sit in a chair for hours. You do regularly need to follow the central message of this book's title – Walk!

Ben Fogle

Ben Fogle, president of the Campaign for National Parks, leading a walk to celebrate the designation of the South Downs as a National Park. (Anne Purkiss, South Downs Joint Committee)

by SIR CHRIS BONINGTON

There are many reasons why the content of this fascinating and thought-provoking book could scarcely be closer to my heart.

No matter how many of the world's great peaks you have climbed, there has always been something wonderfully rewarding about coming home. I have lived in Cumbria since 1974 and so "home" has long been associated with the lovely hills and outstanding scenery of the Lake District.

Here is related how so much is owed to Wordsworth – "one of the first great European writers to advocate walking as a poetic, almost philosophical experience". Nowadays he is irretrievably linked with "golden daffodils", but his pioneer walking tour of the Alps when scarcely out of his teens and his stirring account of an epic ascent from Locarno should appeal to all mountaineers. By the time he was 65 he had incredibly walked an estimated 175,000 miles – mainly across his native Lakeland fells.

Here too is the full context of Wordsworth's plea that the Lake District should be seen as "a sort of national property, in which every man has a right and interest, who has an eye to perceive and a heart to enjoy". Way ahead of its time, it was a brilliant vision of what would later become National Parks. It certainly inspired the hyper-energetic Lakeland clergyman, Canon Rawnsley, to play a key part in setting up the National Trust with its major aim of creating open spaces for freedom to walk. I am a passionate advocate of both conservation and access to the countryside. This book brings into sharp focus just how long and tortuous was the road to achieve this state of affairs; it is up to us all to make sure that we do not lose what has taken such a long time, and an enormous effort, to achieve.

This deeply informative text rightly concludes that "walking was an activity fundamental to Wordsworth's whole being". The same could be said of a more recent and revered personality described as "crusty, eccentric yet delightful … who has become an icon of the long-distance walking movement in Britain". This could only be a reference to Alfred Wainwright, whose "pictorial guides" to the Lakeland Fells have the same enduring cult status as the classic Coast to Coast Walk that he created through the Lake District, Yorkshire Dales and North York Moors.

Long-distance walks rightly have a chapter of their own in this absorbing book, which covers vastly more than my own beloved Lakeland. It embraces such wide-ranging themes as past battles for access, the right to roam, a need to develop urban walks and the future role of walking-based lifestyles. Those of us who have reached a certain age are bound to take notice of the chapter on walking for health. It is a subject that has suddenly come to the fore, with many claims being made on the advantages of a daily walk.

One of the most startling findings has come from the USA, where scientists now believe that walking can improve our mental health. A recent report cites evidence that such activity may protect the brain against shrinking and preserve memory in the elderly. Neurologists who monitored three hundred volunteers over a period of thirteen years found that scans of those who walked nine miles a week had larger brains than those who walked less!

They may be right, yet somehow I can't help but give more credence to the five words set down some two millennia ago by the Greek physician Hippocrates: "Walking is man's best medicine." It says it all.

Sir Chris Bonington

1. WHY WALK?

I have met but with one or two persons in the course of my life who have understood the art of Walking – Thoreau

Walking is what we all do. To walk is to be a human. Walking is the most natural, simplest activity of our species, something we master within a few months of our birth and enjoy, if we are reasonably lucky, until the end of our lives.

And yet, if recent statistics from UK National Statistics Travel Surveys are to be believed, it's an activity which is dying out, at least in modern, prosperous Britain. Between 1993 and 2003, the number of walking "trips" – short journeys outside the home made by British people on foot – declined by a massive 20%. These trips have largely been replaced by journeys by car.

Theoretically, at least, if such trends were to continue, by 2053 pedestrians would have totally disappeared from our towns and cities, as well as from our countryside. This is of course an absurdity. For lots of reasons, some of which are explored in this book, such trends are extremely unlikely to continue.

But if these figures sound like a wild exaggeration, have a look at any old photographs of any small country town you could name, say from early or even the middle of last century.

Apart from the physical changes to the buildings and roads, in most cases by far the biggest change is in the number of people visible walking on the streets. They spill out from the pavements onto the roads, they rush about their business, shop, stroll, loiter, gossip. If it's early in the last century, such vehicles as there are likely to be seen are muscle powered, horse drawn or even hand carts, with horse manure a constant hazard if you crossed the cobbled streets. Until the 1920s a motor-powered car or lorry was a rare sight.

Compare that with a photograph taken in the early 21st century. Such pedestrians as there are in towns, much fewer in total numbers, are squeezed onto narrow pavements, whilst the main streets are now barely visible, crowded with traffic and parked cars. Away from pedestrianised town centres and car parks, into the suburbs and fringe areas, pedestrians virtually disappear, just the occasional hardy soul walking a dog.

The statistics bear this out. In 1986 the average adult in the UK walked an estimated 390km (244 miles) per year. But by 2002 this had declined to a mere 302km (189 miles) per year. That's an average of only 5.8km or 3.6 miles per week.

This represents perhaps one of the most significant, and profound social changes in British history. Greater personal disposable incomes and the rise of affordable personal mechanised transport, mean that the overwhelming majority of adults in the UK are now able to own and run their own car.

Never has the cost of motoring, in real terms, been as low as it is in Britain in the first decade of the 21st century. By 2002 73% of all households in the UK had a car, and 28% had two or more cars. More people now live in two-car households than live in households without a car. Inevitably these car-less households include the many elderly, housebound people who have never driven either because they are the declining survivors of the pre-mass-motoring age, or who, because of age or infirmity, can no longer drive.

Because many are single people living alone, and because larger households are more likely to have at least one car available, the RAC estimate that in fact 81% of people in Britain now live in a household where there is a car available. However it is important to remember that having a car available in a household does not necessarily mean that a particular individual has regular access to that car, which may be exclusively used by the main wage earner.

But National Travel Statistics also confirm that once you have a car in your household, the amount of walking you do – including walks to the nearest bus stop or railway station - declines significantly. People without cars walk an average of 424km

(265 miles) per year, but once a car is acquired this slumps to a meagre 261km or 163 miles, a mere 5.02km or 3.1 miles per week. Middle-aged males driving a company car are the most sedentary of all, walking a mere 221km or 131 miles a year on average. Walking now accounts for only 3% of all distance travelled in the UK.

But if you look at the actual numbers of journeys people make, rather than distance travelled, the statistics are not quite so bleak. 25% of all journeys are still made on foot. 78% of journeys of less than one mile (1.6km) are made on foot, so people still walk to the shops or for a newspaper, or from the car park to the shops, albeit the average length of trip now being just 1km or 0.6 miles – a 15 minute stroll. A mere 6% of walking trips are over 2 miles or 3km.

Does this mean that walking is an outdated, irrelevant travel mode? Should we not accept the fact that Homo sapiens are in the process of evolving to Homo automobiliensis, that in a couple of millennia the first child might be born with a left clutch pedal instead of a residual foot?

Not quite.

Even within human history, let alone human evolution, the car age is a recent, extraordinary, and in world terms almost certainly a brief and localised phenomenon. Most human beings in the 21st century living outside the privileged West still rely on walking as their prime mode of transport, despite the unprecedented rush to industrialisation and motorisation now taking place in the Third World.

But walking is what our bodies have physically evolved to do. Recent archaeological discoveries in Dmanisi, in Georgia, have uncovered remains of what are believed to be tool-making, intelligent creatures some 1.8 million years old who were highly efficient walkers and runners – ancestors of the first real humans, Homo Erectus.

Walking therefore is built into our genetic structure. The human body is superbly evolved to allow us to move on two feet over undulating terrain with speed and ease, to climb mountains,

Walking – a natural human activity.

cross rivers, forests and plains. Our binocular vision enables us to judge distances and threats from our walking and standing position. We can also walk over quite extraordinary distances – not as fast as the larger mammals, but by keeping up steady pace over a long period, say 5 kilometres or 3 miles an hour for several hours, we can cover considerable distances in a day and even more in a week, crossing countries and even continents. As our migrating ancestors proved, our strong, adaptable bodies are capable of swimming rivers, climbing steep hillsides and crags, crossing mountain ranges.

Throughout human history, walking has therefore been a prime mode of transport to find new hunting grounds or new areas to clear and settle, or to conquer and control. Even in relatively recent history, armies have covered prodigious distances on foot. Roman soldiers were expected to march 18 miles in just five hours during each day, carrying full kit and armour. In 1066 the Anglo-Saxon King, Harold Godwinson marched his troops over 200 miles in four days from London to Stamford Bridge to defeat a Viking army, before being finally defeated by William the Conqueror after his army had completed a further equally exhausting march back south to Hastings.

Until the emergence of cheap mechanised travel – steam railways – in the mid 19th century, it was only a minority of the population of Britain who could go anywhere except on foot, or at best with a slow, lumbering carrier's cart over quite appalling unsurfaced roads. Horses were available only to the relatively wealthy. Travel in the relative comfort of a private coach was for the elite. Even a journey inside or even outside a horse-drawn public stagecoach was still beyond the means of most

Mathematician and teacher John Dawson of Sedbergh, who walked to Edinburgh and London to pursue his education.

working people.

People made long journeys on foot which most inhabitants of modern Britain would find unbelievable. When the brilliant shepherd-mathematician John Dawson, born in Garsdale, near Sedbergh, Cumbria, in 1734, decided to study medicine at Edinburgh University, he saved up his earnings from shepherding and hand-knitting in the form of gold sovereigns which were sewn into the lining of his coat. He then walked over the fells from Sedbergh to Edinburgh where he could live in cheap lodgings and survive on oats in the form of porridge in order to be able to attend lectures.

He made a similar journey for further training as a surgeon to London, walking along what were mainly dusty roads but with sections of better maintained turnpike, and getting a lift on carriers' carts where he was able to do so.

This was how ordinary people travelled before the coming of the railways. Even when railway lines were built, and well into the 20th century before local bus services were near universal, poorer rural people were perfectly happy to walk several miles, in all weathers, to the nearest country railway station.

It was only in the late 19th century when suburban railways, electric trams and horse and later motor buses soon allowed people to live in the suburbs of towns rather than in rows of terraced cottages, built alongside the smoky factories or foundries they served. However dwellers in the new suburbs were now largely dependent on motorised transport, rather than walking to access employment, shops and town centre services. People living in rural areas away from the railways had to depend on horse-drawn coaches or waggonettes from the nearest station. It was some time before horse-drawn and finally petrol powered buses ran from the nearest stations. But for most people, there was no choice but to walk.

The coming of the horseless carriage, from its very beginning a symbol of social status and financial success, gave unprecedented freedom and travel opportunity to those who, in the early years of the 20th century, were a privileged and affluent minority. But in the decades after World War I, car ownership rapidly spread throughout society as a car became the ultimate status symbol and icon of personal success. But this also meant that even among ordinary people, walking soon became a low status activity, something which indicated you were poor, unsuccessful, in modern parlance "a loser". Among a majority of British people, that attitude has hardly changed.

Low status for walking is by no means a new phenomenon. Even in the 18th century anyone who could afford to ride a horse looked down literally as well as figuratively on the humble pedestrian. The German author and essayist, Karl Philipp Moritz (1756-1793), made a visit to London in 1782 and walked to the Peak District and back to visit Peak Cavern. Whilst in Continental Europe it was normal for tourists to be seen covering long distances on foot, in England, "a land of carriages and horses", he was a curiosity, a creature of pity or contempt:

Karl Philipp Moritz

George Walker's classic book *The Costume of Yorkshire*, first published in 1814, included a colour plate of a Moor Guide. His clothing is very similar to that worn by most walkers in the early nineteenth century.

A traveller on foot in this country seems to be considered as a sort of wild man or an out-of-the-way being who is stared at, pitied, suspected and shunned by everybody that meets him.
... in England any person undertaking so long a journey on foot is sure to be looked upon and considered as either a beggar, or a vagabond, or some necessitous wretch, which is a character not much more popular than that of a rogue.

Some walkers may feel that little has changed. It was the dramatist Congreve who allegedly invented the popular term "Shank's Mare" or "Shank's Pony", which became the jocular term for walking used by anyone who had no choice but to walk.

And for most British people in the 21st century this perception remains true. Walking is something you do only when there is no other choice. The very word "pedestrian" has overtones of something which is dull,

There is no better way of experiencing the scale and majesty of a coastal cliff landscape than on foot. This splendid stretch of coastal scenery is south of Cayton, near Scarborough.

Walking is companionship – a group of walkers enjoy the view across the South Pennines close to Top Withens, Brontë Moors.

plodding, not very bright. The fast and convenient car has now become the default mode of travel for every conceivable type of journey outside the most congested city centres, except by those too young, old, poor or unfit to be able to drive – or that tiny minority of people too stubborn or eccentric to own a car.

This perception has, in many ways, helped to contribute to the now familiar growth of two, three and even four car households, especially in rural England. This has resulted in a massive expansion of motorisation among the UK population, leading to the current figure of 31 million private cars now (2010) on Britain's roads. But even this is not the anticipated upper limit of the numbers of cars expected to be squeezed onto the road network. The UK is still not yet at saturation point. The total number of registered cars in the UK is anticipated to grow to between 37 and 44 million by 2020 (source RAC Foundation 2008) when presumably virtually every able-bodied adult over 18 years of age will have a car parked in their drive or (somewhere) on the congested street outside their home.

Apart from the massive physical changes that have been made to Britain's towns and countryside to accommodate this huge avalanche of metal, rubber and glass, the impact on individual travel choice has been virtually to eliminate most of what might be described as "utilitarian" walking, that is most walking for all but the shortest distances to work, shops or for business purposes. For most people a walk is simply something you have to do, to get from your armchair to your garage or parked car outside your front door, or when you arrive from the car park at your destination to the shop, office, restaurant or visitor attraction which is the purpose of your journey. Indeed if you can't park your vehicle as close as possible to that final destination, then anger and irritation is likely to result, so conditioned are we to easy motorised access to every place we choose. Walking is effort, walking is being exposed to the elements such as wind, rain and cold, away from the air-conditioned sanctuary and security of the car. Walking is being exposed to other people. It's something most people want to do as little as possible.

But that isn't quite the end of the story. For centuries walking has been undertaken for other reasons than for purely utilitarian journeys, but as a prime leisure activity. As we shall see, this is something deeply related to our cultural history, a complex response to the many challenges and pressures of industrial civilisation, mental as well as physical.

To some extent walking for pleasure has now become a rejection of the consumerist values of modern society, a re-assertion of older values, something more than mere escapism. Leisure walking is a physical activity, one in which the journey on foot is an end in itself. The destination is less important than the process of getting there – indeed it may not be relevant. "Going for a walk" implies that the activity itself is what matters. It is a sport, not in the narrow, highly commercialised, competitive sense of what we normally now understand as "sport", but nevertheless physical activity for its own sake, to enjoy the process of action, of being alive.

It can be a quite vigorous activity – a long and energetic walk, climbing hills at a sharp pace, and is close to its sister activities of running, jogging, or in the countryside, cross-country or fell running.

But walking has also long been a competitive sport in the normally accepted sense. There is a separate, long established tradition of "race walking" along public roads, the "heel and toe" events which are carefully regulated. Interestingly enough, this was a sport which originated in the 17th and 18th centuries by upper class gentlemen who did not, of course, walk themselves but placed wagers on their footmen to race along the "turnpikes, heaths, downs and race courses of England". Race meetings were organised that could last up to 24 hours and even, one recorded event, six days.

Wagers were huge, not only at public competitive events, but for individual walking feats. In 1809 Captain Robert Barclay Allardice, a prodigious walker reputedly capable of walking up to 60 miles a day, took on a challenge to walk one mile every hour for 1,000 hours - just under 42 days - to cover 1,000 miles over Newmarket Heath for a wager of £1,000 guineas, which he duly did. It is said that more than £100,000 was taken in bets for

Captain Robert Barclay Allardice 1779-1854 – a prodigious walker.

the event. This was only one of Barclay's many incredible walking feats.

By the mid 19th century "pedestrianism", as it became known, had spread down the social orders with many clubs and associations being formed throughout Europe and America to encourage the sport. The first Amateur Walking Championships were held in 1866. By 1904 Race Walking was part of the Olympic Games and the national Road Walking Association was formed in 1906 to regulate the sport in the UK with suitable approved rules and regulations. Whilst the growth of motor traffic even along country lanes has made road walking as such a far less pleasant and safe activity than it used to be, "power walking" remains an extremely popular and challenging sporting activity, including within cities such as London.

But enjoyable and worthwhile as race walking and competitive marathon, fell or cross country running may be as a physical activity, less vigorous, non-competitive leisure walking is a quite different if equally valid outdoor sport activity. The prime difference is that physical activity and exertion, though important, does not dominate the experience to the same degree.

There are other equally important aspects of slower-paced, "gentle" leisure walking, to be enjoyed and even savoured. There is the physical beauty of a landscape, or equally enjoyable in a different way, a cityscape with different forms of architecture and man-made structures, the rich variety of Georgian or Victorian townscapes. There is the visual experience of the natural world – greenery, wildlife, botany, the subtle colour changes of the weather seasons, cloudscapes. Or maybe it's about being able to perceive and unravel the human and cultural dimension of a landscape, the complex patterns of dry stone walls, ancient hedges, old field systems, canal sides, industrial remains, ancient track ways, old farmsteads and barns.

Walking is a sensory experience. Interacting with the external environment, it brings all your five senses into play – the wind on your face or in your hair, the sting of rain or snow, the feel of rock or moss against your hand, the smell of rotting autumn leaves, of pine woods, of summer gorse blossom, the catching of light on the surface of a river or lake, the sound of a curlew on a moorland or rooks in high trees, of wind rustling through trees or in reeds, the crunch of boots on gravel. Even taste can be involved – the salt taste of the sea in a coastal storm or bilberries or blackberries gathered in late summer or autumn.

Walking reconnects the walker with the natural world, the eco-system within which we live and breathe, the wider environment which supports us as living organisms and on which ultimately we depend for our existence.

But a walk may equally well be about companionship with one or more other people, or even a group, where conversation, shared ideas and empathy, time spent together, is the focus of the experience, whether with parent, child, lover, partner, or just friend or acquaintance. Or even that least complaining but most devoted of companions, a dog. Walking is a social experience.

This is where the gentle art of walking begins to emerge as a key human activity. Slower walking can often be a more intense experience than the exhilarating fast hike or run through the countryside, if the real aim of the activity is to absorb the special qualities of the environment through which you are passing. It's about ensuring you have time to pause, to look or listen more intensely at what is there to be seen and heard and felt. To paraphrase the late Eric Schumacher, "Slow is Beautiful" when it comes to fully experiencing what the countryside and the town has to offer the quiet and observant traveller.

Nevertheless, a good walk also blends enough reasonably vigorous activity to get blood circulating, lungs working, the fine sense of well-being that comes from steady exercise, with sufficient time to look, feel, observe, maybe pausing on a hilltop to absorb a view, or in a woodland copse to observe the unfolding of a fern or wood anemone.

Tranquillity is another quality of the countryside which walkers are best able to enjoy. Despite the constant blight of traffic noise, and in increasing numbers of places aircraft noise, there are still countless places even in crowded Britain where you can enjoy tranquillity. Apart from footsteps, breathing and the occasional disturbed pebble or snapped twig, walking is a near silent activity. This means the natural world is less easily disturbed, and sounds such as birdsong or running water are not drowned out. It is also easier on foot to observe wildlife at close quarters, though being stationary to listen and watch is invariably the best way to do so.

Above all, walking is an activity where the various sensory perceptions blend, build up within the mind and memory a special and unique sense of place. This is more than just the character of a landscape, but a mixture of elusive qualities that gave a place its own identity. Much depends on the time of day, the season, the weather, the subtle changes and moods of light, sounds, scent and smells, the lie of the land and texture of path or soil against your feet. It can also be about a sense of history or of personal associations of a particular or special location. All these factors combine to create a sense of a place, something which is hard to define in language because it can only be experienced on foot, through alerted senses.

Some people even feel they have never been to a place until they have actually walked there, preferably for at least a whole day or longer. Drive through a stretch of countryside and it's little more real than being in front of a television screen, dominated (especially for the driver) by the monotony of a tarmac strip and the tail lights of the vehicle ahead, a fleeting, de-sensitised, high speed glimpse of what is beyond the windscreen, and accessible by only one, somewhat deprived, of your five senses. Buses are a little better because you gain in height and are able to see over walls and hedges, and generally travel more slowly.

But no mechanised transport – though cycling comes very close – can match the special experience of walking where for a short time at least, you become part of your surroundings, at one with the environment.

Walking can therefore restore that sense of proportion and scale of a landscape that we have largely destroyed with high speed travel along motorways or high-speed rail lines. Climb a hill on foot and you have a real sense of the size, steepness and massiveness of the hill compared with your minute sense of self. Cross a ridge from one valley into the next and you have a unique sense of the massive geological forces that have shaped and carved out that landscape. Walk over an empty, wind-swept Pennine moor, miles from human habitation, where you are alone with the elements enjoying a sense of space and emptiness even in modern, over populated Britain, and you begin to realise how marginal and temporary man's domination of his environment actually is. Coastal walking can also give a sense of the vastness and elemental power of the sea. This is most notable in areas such as Pembrokeshire, Cornwall, the North York Moors and even the Sussex Downs where mighty cliffs pounded by angry seas give insight into the infinite power of natural forces so easily forgotten in modern urban living.

The lone walker experiences a physical closeness to the natural world.

Walking is also about space in another sense – space to think, to be oneself. Nothing quite beats solitary walking to give an opportunity to let worries, problems, stress, ideas work their way through the conscious and even unconscious mind, so that what seemed an intractable problem has, by the end of the walk, been absorbed within a wider perspective, and perhaps even been resolved.

You don't need a long day walking in the hills to achieve this. Even a short, easy walk can give sufficient mental space to clarify ideas and discover creative solutions to whatever mental challenges you face. If you visit Charles Darwin's home at Down House, at Downe in Kent, you will find at the end of the garden the short 100-metre stroll by tall hedges known as The Sand Walk. This is where Darwin paced up and down whilst resolving many intractable problems, challenges and insights when writing one of the greatest and most influential scientific works of all time, *On The Origin of Species*. Darwin's therapeutic walks, undertaken at intervals between intensive writing sessions in his study, were for him a vital part of the creative process. Equally it was his own local walks in the fields around the village of Downe and on the nearby North Downs which inspired many insights into natural selection. Many other writers, scientists and philosophers have used walking as an aid to thinking and new ideas.

Inevitably, walking with other people dilutes the

intensity of the thinking process. Interaction between people changes the focus of the experience. Yet two people who know each other well can share feelings about external experiences and communicate those feelings on a walk, silently, almost imperceptibly, with hardly a word spoken. Such shared experience can be intensified by the presence of someone on your own emotional wavelength.

On the other hand, the happy chatter of a group of walkers can quickly scare away wildlife for miles around, and rapidly undermine any sense of tranquillity. One disadvantage of walking with a group or club is the social experience of companionship and friendly gossip soon becomes the real focus of the walk, the landscape and natural beauty reduced to just the background. There's nothing wrong with that in itself – walking with friends is essentially a social experience, and highly enjoyable, but it is a different kind of experience to that enjoyed by the solitary walker or thoughtful couple.

But walking is also a means to enjoy other outdoor activities. Traditionally all the great naturalists and geologists of the 19th and early 20th centuries were also keen walkers. "Field

A lone walker enjoys a sense of space and wilderness near Esk Head, Lake District National Park. (Dorian Speakman)

Charles Darwin – walking inspired his creative thinking process.

work" implies being out there with boots and a rucksack. There is a long and distinguished history of painters and photographers who were also keen walkers. A sketchbook or camera in the rucksack not only captures memories of a walk, but the walk itself is the means to access key locations for the painting or the photograph. For the photographer, judging ideal times of day and light conditions may require long pauses in a walk to capture the moment. Many painters use photographs as an aide-memoire, to distil landscape forms, shapes and colours in the memory, though the final results may be a long way from the exact, literal realism of a photograph.

Urban walking is also the best way to enjoy fine architecture within a town or city setting, as we shall suggest in Chapter 6. Historians visiting a battlefield, or area of town or countryside of particular historic interest or importance, inevitably need to do so on foot. Gardens and art historians wanting to explore a historic landscape garden must walk through it to enjoy their particular activity. Even golfers sometimes claim that their enjoyment of a round of golf in a spectacular setting comes as much from the walk between the greens as in the competitive element of the sport.

This is all as it should be and emphasises the growing importance of leisure walking as a part of our culture. But it is also true to suggest that people who walk reasonable distances, regularly, for pleasure, whether in a walking club or on their own, are likely to develop a way of thinking, which reflects shared values as well as physical fitness.

If someone says "she's or he's a great walker" one knows instinctively that they'll have certain values and attitudes to the countryside, to natural beauty, to access, to the environment, that you know and can share, even though on other matters, for example politics or religion, you may have very different views and perceptions. That matters not. What is important is that shared culture, a culture which has been learned and absorbed from many different sources. They are also likely to be highly knowledgeable about favourite walking areas, Scotland, the Lake District, Wales, about "their" special bit of the British Isles.

Particularly in the North of England, these shared values cut across class and income boundaries. You will often find people from modest backgrounds with a passion for walking and a deep knowledge of the countryside, of long distance footpaths and trails, and about their nearest piece of countryside where again their local knowledge of footpaths and routes is sometimes astonishing.

This has nowhere been better expressed than by the author J B Priestley in his *English Journey* published in 1934. Writing about his native Bradford he noted the intimate, almost symbiotic relationship that existed in the 1930s between the working people of industrial Bradford and the nearby Yorkshire Dales:

Everybody was knowledgeable about the Dales and their walks, and would spend hours discussing the minutest details of them. You caught the fever when you were quite young and it never left you. However small and dark your office or warehouse was, somewhere inside your head the high moors were glowing, the curlews were crying, and there blew a wind as soft as it came straight from the middle of the Atlantic. This is why we did not care very much if our city had no charm, for it was simply a place to go and work in, until it was time to set out for Wharfedale or Wensleydale again.

But as Priestley hints, and as we shall explore in the next chapter, even in working class communities such as those within Bradford, there were powerful literary influences at work:

We were all, at heart, Wordsworthians to a man … ..we have Wordsworth in our very legs.

This passion for and identification with a nearby National Park or special area of countryside as a place to escape to and to walk in, still exists in many Northern and Midland communities – Leeds and Bradford primarily look to the Dales; Manchester, Derby and Sheffield and Nottingham to the Peak District; Hull, Darlington and

J B Priestley in characteristic pipe-smoking pose. He was well aware of how Bradford's working people had a passion for walking in the Yorkshire Dales. (Special Collections, Bradford University Library)

Middlesbrough to the North York Moors; Newcastle to Northumberland and the Cheviots; Liverpool to Snowdonia; and Liverpool, Manchester and Preston to the Lake District.

This reflects long-standing traditions in these communities of some clear strands in our culture, based on transport links, rail and road, especially the Victorian railways from town and city centres into that countryside. In other areas of Britain, most notably in London and the South East, the love of the countryside may take different and more diffuse forms – though areas such as the North Downs and the Chilterns have some of the same close links with walkers from London as do the Peak and Dales with northern cities, whilst areas such as the mountains of the Lake District and Snowdonia and the Scottish Highlands have always had a more national appeal.

This relationship with special areas of countryside has two key elements, both closely linked to walking. The first is perceived access to those landscapes, as green open spaces, places of natural beauty that contrast with the less attractive, crowded urban environments where most people live and work – though such areas also urgently need protection and improvement. Access has several elements – physical access, in most cases by private car or by public road or rail transport from home to the area in question, and then accessibility of that area on foot along the footpath network or across open areas of countryside or shoreline. Finally there is intellectual access, which is about people being able to understand and being motivated to get out and enjoy what these areas have to offer the walker.

The second element is protection of those landscapes, which from the 19th century onwards have been increasingly vulnerable to industrial and residential developments. Access to the countryside is meaningless if that countryside has been destroyed by thoughtless, unsightly and threatening development.

The long campaign for a carefully protected, fully accessible British countryside is a story of how the ideas and convictions of a relatively small number of people – poets, painters, visionaries, protesters, campaigners, and finally legislators – have triumphed to a remarkable degree. Though inevitably there have been losses along the way, at least many of our finest areas of countryside are now protected and fully accessible in ways which would have been unimaginable two generations ago.

Whilst National Parks, and both international and national governments' protection of nature, are now a worldwide phenomenon, the central idea of the restorative powers of the natural world owes much to ideas generated by a small group of writers and thinkers in late 18th and early 19th century Britain. Percy Bysshe Shelley was right to suggest that "poets are the unacknowledged legislators of the world."

It was the experience of walking in the countryside which, more than anything else, inspired this worldwide conservation movement.

2. WALKING AND THE ROMANTIC IMAGINATION

Drive my dead thoughts over the universe

Like withered leaves to quicken a new birth!

And by the incantation of this verse,

Scatter as from an unextinguished hearth

Ashes and sparks, my words among mankind!

– Shelley

During the late 18th and early 19th centuries, a profound cultural change swept across Europe. This change was fuelled by many factors – the growing industrial revolution, which started in Britain and was soon to sweep across other parts of Europe as "manufactories" - first water, and then steam powered mills – were built in the valleys and along the new canals of Wales, the Scottish lowlands, the Cotswolds, the Midlands and the Pennines. New industry created new wealth, a new middle class in the rapidly growing manufacturing towns, ports and cities of Britain. Outside Britain there was a collapse of the "ancient regimes" of feudal Europe, ignited by the writings of men like Voltaire, Rousseau, Tom Paine, whose book *The Rights of Man* (1791) became a world-wide bestseller, a stimulus for the American Revolution. Above all was the French Revolution of 1789 itself, the overturning of all established order, with horrific consequences and social upheaval which terrified the British governing classes for generations.

Art reflected these dramatic social and economic changes. The old, now stilted neo-classical forms and conventional, stereotypical imagery in art and literature, and rigid structures of music were increasingly rejected. A new emotionalism – a love of the strange, the bizarre, the Gothic, the picturesque, the sublime, were the fashion. It was a period of change, a rejection of old, established values, a period of experiment, of new forms and new emotions, from the daring new harmonies of Haydn's Creation to Beethoven's late quartets, from Blake's visionary engravings to Constable's meticulous recording of weather, colour and light in lowland landscapes and Turner's visionary explorations of form, light, power and shape in mountains which were to anticipate the Impressionist movement.

Constable and Turner were only two of the greatest of the many artists to discover the power of landscape both in Britain and abroad, to create a new taste for the picturesque. It was clergyman, author and artist William Gilpin (1724-1804) who first popularised the concept of the "picturesque" – landscape perceived as conforming to certain accepted rules of symmetry and taste to form a picture – which was to influence the work of many artists and writers working at the end of the 18th and early years of the 19th century.

The brilliant water colourist Thomas Girtin (1775-1802) died tragically young but had a profound impact on English painting. Turner, his close friend, commented, "had he lived I would have starved". John Sell Cotman (1782-1842) of Norwich was another extraordinary fine water colourist whose observations of the natural world and of architecture were to have a lasting impression on the Romantic movement. But above all it was Joseph Mallord William Turner (1775-1851) whose artistic impressions of journeys through the Alps and through so many of the upland landscapes of "picturesque" Britain were to create a new taste for wilder and more rugged landscapes. He recorded his extensive travels – on horseback – in both oil and watercolours, and subsequently many popular engravings. All express the dramatic, epic power of nature – storms, sunsets, darkness, colour, light and man's insignificance – that has become central to our visual understanding and experience of our greatest landscapes. We see much of the landscapes of what are now our National Parks and protected

J M W Turner's famous painting of Semerwater in the Yorkshire Dales, completed in 1817-18. (British Museum)

areas of countryside through the eyes of these great artists and of their many successors, photographers as well as painters.

But the power of written language was equally as important. In England, it was William Wordsworth (1770-1850) who first and most convincingly embodied that new radical vision, experimenting with (and soon rejecting) ideas of pantheism and revolution, before exploring the inner world of the imagination and feelings. With his friend and later rival Samuel Taylor Coleridge he published the celebrated *Lyrical Ballads* of 1799, developing a new, sparse poetical style and subject matter that focused on the feelings and experiences of ordinary country people, rejecting the highly conventional, artificial forms and neo-classical themes of most 18th century poetry.

The Romantics, by which term Wordsworth and his followers and successors came to be known, were deeply concerned with individual experience. Romantic writing is essentially about the personal,

William Wordsworth on Helvellyn 1842 – painted by B R Haydon when the poet was 72.

even egotistical artist perceiving the beauty, vastness and meaning of the universe, questioning the establishment's view of the natural order of things, an ordered universe which leading geologists and astronomers, well before Darwin, were increasingly beginning to undermine with concepts about the universe and its history that were both dynamic and dangerous.

Ennerdale Water engraved by William Westall in 1822. Westall (1781-1850) first visited the Lake District in 1811 and spent part of every winter there for the next nine years. He became a close friend of both Robert Southey and the Wordsworths. In 1820 he married Ann Sedgwick of Dent, sister of the famous geologist Professor Adam Sedgwick. The engraving includes a lone person heading towards the lake.

But Wordsworth was also one of the first great European writers to advocate leisure walking as a poetic, almost philosophical experience, as a means of communicating directly with the natural world. Because he grew up in the Lake District, it was his evolution as a poet in those mountains – the growth of a poet's mind – that became the theme of *The Prelude* (1805), one of the first poems in the English language to explore the concept of the imagination, as it develops and matures through childhood experience into an adult's more complex philosophical awareness.

Walking was an activity fundamental to Wordsworth's whole being. His friend and admirer Thomas De Quincey calculated that by the time he was 65, Wordsworth must have walked an estimated 175,000-180,000 miles, mainly across his native Lakeland fells of which he had an intimate, walker's knowledge.

But his rambles were not confined to Cumbria. In 1790, aged just 20, he undertook one of the first recorded extended walking tours in northern Europe, to France, Italy, Switzerland and Germany, spending two months with his Cambridge friend Robert Jones. It was a time when taking such a tour on foot (apart from using a rowing boat for a short section of the Rhine) was still considered to be eccentric, even a little dangerous. Wealthy young men, even many years afterwards, inevitably took the grand tour of mainland Europe in a carriage or on horseback and with servants.

Something of the experience on that pioneering walking tour, much of it done "at marching pace", was to find its way, 15 years later, into Book VI of *The Prelude*. Wordsworth gives a detailed description of an epic ascent from Locarno, with all the intensity of feeling of any mountain guidebook of the ensuing two centuries. The companions get lost and have to ask the way from a local peasant who directs them along a river valley and into a "gloomy pass" with:

The torrents shooting from the clear blue sky,
The rocks that mutter'd close upon our ears,
Black drizzling crags that spake by the wayside
As if a voice were in them.....;

The wild scenery of Alpine landscapes for Wordsworth hinted at something greater than humankind, symbols of "Eternity", beyond the comprehension of mere mankind, in his youth at least, almost a vision of a Pantheistic force in nature.

Wordsworth was by no means unique in seeking and finding the sublime in mountains, in the unfettered forces of nature, but he differed from most writers of his generation, by basing his writing on close observation of nature, and on recalling experiences of the specific moments or "spots" of time which have a profound effect on our emotional development.

Many commentators have noted that much of this power of observation came from the close intellectual and emotional relationship with his sister Dorothy, his companion on so many walks and trips well into middle life and his marriage. Dorothy, until her last years, was also a keen and energetic walker, at a time when women walking on their own in the countryside were regarded as somewhat suspect figures. But her keen observations of the natural world, many superbly recalled in her Journals, provided the inspiration for some great poetry. She was also William's amanuensis and scribe, preparing final copies of his poems ready for publication, but also his inspiration. In many of her *Journals*, brief observations, clearly shared and discussed on their walks together, find their way into her brother's poems. Most famously, on April 15th 1802 her *Journal* recalls on one of their walks seeing wild daffodils by Gowbarrow on Ullswater:

Dorothy Wordsworth.

I never saw daffodils so beautiful they grew among the mossy stones about and about them, some rested their heads upon the stones as on a pillow for weariness and the rest tossed and reeled and danced and seemed as if they verily laughed with the wind that blew upon them over the lake, they looked so gay, ever glancing and changing ......

These observations were later transformed by William into the celebrated lines "I wandered lonely as a Cloud" once recited by every schoolchild, an example of that typical Wordsworthian "spot of time", of insight and pleasure, the repeating image of the dancing daffodils that "flash upon the inward eye which is the bliss of solitude".

It was the ability to transform a particular experience into something universal that made Wordsworth one of the giants of the Romantic movement, but his strength lay, in his greatest work, in re-creating that sense of a real experience of the natural world. At the heart of this experience was the act of walking.

In one of his most powerful poems, *Resolution and Independence*, sometimes referred to as The Leech Gatherer, there is a magnificent description of a morning walk after a storm where:

– on the moors
the hare is running races in her mirth;
And with her feet she from the plashy earth
Raises a mist, that glittering in the sun,
Runs with her all the way, wherever she does run.

This description is something that only a frequent walker on the moors, who has observed such a phenomenon, could describe the running hare in such a way, with the evocative word "plashy" evoking the feel of a rain-soaked moor better than a paragraph of prose. But this precedes a remarkable meeting. It is on this moor that the neurotic, depressed poet meets a frail, dignified old man who appears almost as part of the landscape,

as a huge stone is sometimes seen to lie,
Couched on the bald top of an eminence.

– searching for leeches for use in medicine. There were still a few left in the moorland ponds or tarns to be found to support his meagre income:

In my mind's eye I seemed to see him pace
About the dreary moors continually.

But the dignity and courage of the old man facing hopeless odds for survival puts the poet's own neuroses and fears into perspective. The poem – an experience on a moorland walk – becomes a simple and powerful statement about the nobility of man and fundamental goodness and dignity of human nature, a central theme of romantic ideology.

The idea that there should be national protection for our greatest areas of unspoiled countryside has its germ in Wordsworth's own *Guide to the Lakes* first published in 1810. In the closing pages of a later edition of 1835 to this much reprinted guide, he suggested, albeit in an elitist way, that "persons of pure taste" should support his view that the Lake District needed protecting from the harmful influence of new property developers and they should:

deem the district a sort of national property, in which every man has a right and interest, who has an eye to perceive and a heart to enjoy.

Has there ever been any better way of describing the underlying concept and the core objectives of what later would become both the National Trust and Britain's National Parks?

Wordsworth's close but later strained relationship with the intense and brilliant Samuel Taylor Coleridge (1772-1834) had its first flowering, once again on a walking tour that William and Dorothy made in 1797 along the Somerset Coast, during which meeting Coleridge conceived the idea of the epic poem *The Ancient Mariner*. William and Dorothy soon moved to Alfoxeden, on the northern edge of the Quantocks, some three miles from Nether Stowey where Coleridge was living, and the trio spent much time walking, talking and philosophising together. For some heady months they were "three persons and one soul". One result of this close relationship was the publication of *The Lyrical Ballads* which featured *The Ancient Mariner*. But Coleridge's own work gained much in intensity and force from the influence of Wordsworth, including the ability to look at the natural world with Wordsworthian exactness and precision.

The Napoleonic Wars at the end of the 18th and start of the 19th century and consequent dangers of travelling abroad, did much to encourage wealthy travellers to discover their own mountains rather than the Italian or French Alps. It was to the Lake District, Snowdonia and Scotland, still largely undiscovered terrain, that the seekers of the sublime in nature were to extend their travels, especially on foot.

One typical bright young intellectual to be attracted to the Wordsworth-Coleridge circle was

William Hazlitt.

Thomas De Quincey.

William Hazlitt (1778-1930), essayist, art and literary critic. He was so inspired by both Wordsworth's and Coleridge's writings that he deliberately took a walking tour in Wales in 1798 to prepare himself to meet them, before making his way on foot to Nether Stowey to meet Coleridge who he had already met by chance. He described Wordsworth, whom he met for the first time on this visit, as "gaunt and Don Quixote-like" dressed "quaintly" in "a brown fustian jacket and striped pantaloons" with something of "a roll, lunge in his gait".

Hazlitt later joined Coleridge and a local man, John Chester, on a memorable walking tour through Exmoor, walking:

.......for miles and miles on dark brown heaths overlooking the Channel, with the Welsh hills beyond, at times descending into little sheltered valleys close by the seaside with a smuggler's face scowling by us, and then had to ascend conical hills with a path winding through a coppice to a barren top, like a monk's shaven crown, from one of which I pointed out to Coleridge the bare masts of a vessel on the very edge of the horizon, like his own spectre ship in The Ancient Mariner.

Interestingly enough, by the time he was writing his influential essay on the pleasures of walking, *On Going on a Journey* first published in *Table-Talk* in 1822, Hazlitt became, like many later writers, a strong advocate of solitary walking. In words which still reverberate to the modern reader:

I cannot see the wit of walking and talking at the same time..... Give me the clear blue sky over my head, and the green turf beneath my feet, a winding road before me, and three hours' march to dinner – and then to thinking!

Like most of us, Hazlitt was inconsistent. Even in the same essay he concedes that walking whilst talking with Coleridge was something special.

Thomas De Quincey (1795-1859) translator and essayist, now best remembered for his remarkable *Confessions of an Opium Eater* (1821), was another passionate disciple of the Wordsworthian school of walking, mountains and romantic feeling. As an unhappy, sensitive 16 year old at Manchester Grammar school, obsessed with Wordsworth's poetry, he ran away from school to set out, a diminutive figure, walking for several weeks in North Wales, surviving on a guinea a week from a kind uncle, staying in cottages, and occasionally inns, and eating local food. The experience was recalled in very precise detail in his Confessions which also traces his addictions, sadly like his hero Coleridge, with laudanum or opium and also alcohol.

Like many subsequent writers, De Quincey discovered walking a great stimulus to thought:

I have always found it easier to think over a matter of perplexity whilst walking in wide open spaces, under the broad eye of natural heavens, than whilst shut up in a room.

An interesting insight is provided into the way walkers were regarded by inn keepers as some kind of vermin to be treated without any due respect. When arriving late at an inn in Shrewsbury, De Quincey was careful to announce the fact that he was to catch the prestigious Holyhead Night Mail the following morning and:

This character at once installed me as rightful a guest of the inn however profligate a life I might have previously led like a pedestrian.

He was then treated like a lord given every attention. Having walked through mid Wales to Shrewsbury he had decided to use up his last few pounds to take the coach to London to seek his fortune.

But De Quincey was soon drawn back to the mountains, and in 1809 leased Dove Cottage in Grasmere from the Wordsworths, soon becoming one of the elite circle of writers and intellectuals residing in the Lake District at that time.

Up to the end of his life, even through the worst of his opium addiction, De Quincey's sanity and remnants of health were restored by walking. Living in Scotland in his later years, in 1848 he was still able to walk 10 miles from his village near Edinburgh to meet the American writer Ralph Waldo Emerson.

It is true therefore to suggest that the fashion for leisure walking through the countryside in the early 19th century was an activity made fashionable and promoted by a small group of intellectuals of whom Wordsworth and Coleridge were the focus.

Even the sharp and eminently sensible Jane Austen, who brilliantly satirised the fashion for Gothic Horror in her novel *Northanger Abbey*, had many of her feisty heroines such as Marion Dashwood in *Sense and Sensibility*, Elizabeth Bennet in *Pride and Prejudice* or Emma Woodhouse in *Emma*, taking country walks to visit friends or just to enjoy the experience. This was at a time when most leisure walking by upper class ladies was confined to the artificially created "Romantic landscapes" of the great country estates, with their carefully created perspectives and "picturesque" views, complete with mock bridges and even ruins to replicate the fashionable canvases of the best 17th century Italian painters.

Such a feeling for landscape and for exploring it on foot had a profound influence on what might be described as the second generation of romantic poets and thinkers. Percy Bysshe Shelley (1792-1822), romantic, radical and revolutionary, a keen walker from his Oxford years, quickly absorbed the Wordsworthian concept of the "lordliness and grandeur" of mountain scenery, with walking trips into Wales and the Lake District. He often walked the 32 miles from Marlow in Berkshire, where he was living, to London.

Percy Bysshe Shelley.

In 1814 Shelley undertook a rather different kind of walking tour. When tiring of his young wife Harriet, he scandalously eloped with Mary Wollstonecraft (the eventual author of Frankenstein) and her stepsister Jane Clairmont. The three of them undertook an arduous journey from the French coast to Switzerland, Shelley pawning his watch to have sufficient money to buy food and a small donkey for their luggage, which before the end of the trip Shelley ended up having to ride.

Two years later Shelley, now a part-exile because of his atheistic and revolutionary views, was back in Switzerland in 1816 and staying in a villa on the edge of Lake Geneva. His poem *Mont Blanc* written that summer describes the infinite power in the mountains, ravines and glaciers, anticipating generations of mountain worshippers to come. Like Wordsworth, Shelley saw a moral voice in the sublime beauty and awesome majesty of nature:

George Gordon, Lord Byron.

Thou hast a voice, great Mountain, to repeal
Large codes of fraud and woe; not understood
By all, but which the wise, and great, and good
Interpret, or make felt, or deeply feel.

In that same summer of 1816, also staying on the shores of Lake Geneva in the neighbouring Villa Diorati, was another revolutionary figure. George Gordon (1788-1824) better known as Lord Byron. Byron, perhaps the most charismatic and scandalous of all English poets, adventurer, lover, wit, brilliant master of poetic forms, had a huge influence on the emerging taste for wild landscapes not just in Britain, but throughout Europe. His six months stay in the Swiss Alps, including an extended boat trip along Lake Geneva with Shelley, produced some of the most grandiose passages in his verse. This is evident in the Faustian verse drama *Manfred*, where Manfred climbs the Jungfrau to experience the immense, extreme powers of nature by conversing with magical spirits and "alpine witches" who supposedly inhabited the mountain peaks.

But his most influential poem was *Childe Harold's Pilgrimage*, published as a series of cantos between 1812 and 1818. Described as an extensive "travelogue" of Byron's journeys through Italy and the Alps, *Childe Harold* was to inspire not only aristocratic travellers on the Grand Tour to collect the most romantic "sights" of Europe, but future generations of mountaineers and mountain-worshippers:

.... Above me the Alps
The palaces of Nature, whose vast walls
Have pinnacled in clouds their snowy scalps,
And throned Eternity in icy halls,
Of cold sublimity where forms and falls
The avalanche – the thunderbolt of snow!
All that expands the spirit, yet appals,
Gather around these summits, as to show
How earth may pierce to Heaven, yet leave vain man below.

John Keats, born in London in 1795 was also sufficiently inspired by the works of Wordsworth and Coleridge to believe he too needed to undertake a strenuous walking tour of the Lake District and Scotland in 1818. Sadly his constitution was not the strongest, and the experience, which left him overwhelmed with the grandeur of Lakeland and Highlands scenery, may have also contributed to his death as he returned to London after foul weather utterly exhausted. Within months he had contracted the consumption which led to his tragically early death, but may well have helped fuel the intense beauty of his greatest verse.

But perhaps the most remarkable of the slightly later Romantic walker-poets whose work was in total contrast to the grandiose rhetoric of Shelley and Byron, or the rich sensuality of Keats, was the modest Northamptonshire "Peasant Poet" John Clare (1793-1864). Clare differed from the Lakeland poets in a number of fundamental ways. He was a poor man, son of a cottage farmer, and largely self-taught. But though walking for Clare was a necessity not a choice, he absorbed through his reading the Wordsworthian obsession with the natural world, not the mountain landscapes of Cumbria, but like John Constable, lowland England, the ordinary countryside of his native Northamptonshire. He also saw the countryside through the eyes of a countryman, not a

John Clare.

sophisticated townsman, with a knowledge and an understanding of both the natural world and the hardship of rural life at a time of Agricultural Enclosures and dispossession of many commoners. Clare's early work, despite its eccentricities of both spelling and punctuation, was discovered by John Taylor, of the publishing company Taylor and Hessey, publishers of James Thomson's popular *Seasons* that Clare had so much admired.

His first book of poems, published in 1820, was a publishing sensation and rapidly went through four editions. For a brief period Clare was the talk of the town. However, fashions quickly change, and Clare's subsequent book of poems did not sell. Torn between his rural Northamptonshire neighbours that he lived with, who now regarded him as something of an outsider, and his literary admirers in London, and despite some aristocratic patronage, Clare faced devastating poverty for his wife and large family of seven children. These pressures in turn led to mental breakdown and Clare spent the last 27 years of his life in various asylums, though amazingly still able to write some fine poetry.

Few poets have ever written verse of such direct sharp, personal observation of the countryside as John Clare. He was a great walker, and what he saw on his many rural rambles was described with the clear, sharp eye of the countryman, with a remarkable exactness and intensity:

I love at eventide to walk alone,
Down narrow lanes o'erhung with dewy thorn,
Where from the long grass underneath, the snail
Jet-black creeps out and sprouts his timid horn.
(Summer Moods)

One particular northern household where Wordsworth had a huge influence was that of the Reverend Patrick Brontë living in the industrial village of Haworth in the heart of the Yorkshire South Pennines with his gifted children. The children were all keen walkers, none more so than Emily, for whom the wild moorland extending to the far horizons behind the village of Haworth became a potent symbol of personal, creative and sexual freedom. Much of the power of her novel *Wuthering Heights* (1847) comes from the overpowering sense of the wild, open moorland surrounding the two houses – one on the moor top, one in the sheltered valley – where the dramatic events of the novel take place. The intense sense of place of the book came out of Emily's constant energetic walks over the nearby moorland above Haworth and Stanbury, and visits to local moorland farms and grander houses.

Her sister, Charlotte, herself a major novelist, writes movingly of her sister's homesickness when confined to the school at Roe Head where for a few months in 1835 she was a pupil:

Her nature proved too strong for her fortitude. Every morning when she woke, the vision of home and the moors rushed on her, and darkened and saddened the day that lay before her.

The Romantic revolution and discovering of the countryside was by no means confined to British shores. In Germany, the great German poet, playwright, philosopher and statesman Johann Wolfgang von Goethe, in the middle of a severe winter, made a remarkable ascent of the 1142 metre high Brocken summit, the highest point in the Harz mountains of North central Germany. The Brocken is a mountain rich in folklore linked to devils, witches and the celebrated Walpurgisnacht, April 30th, May-Day eve, when the witches and devils come out for their rituals and wild dance. Not only did Goethe use the experience in an evocative poem, *Harzreise in Winter* (Winter Journey to the Harz) but it became the setting for a dramatic central scene in his great poetic drama *Faust*.

It was hardly surprising that The Brocken and in particular the walk to its summit became a focal point for later generations of walkers and romantics, the most famous of these being the lyric poet and radical Heinrich Heine (1797-1856). Heine's *Harzreise* or Harz Journey (1823), describing his own walking trip from Gottingen through the Harz mountains, over the Brocken summit and down the stunningly beautiful Ilsetal valley, soon became a literary classic attracting more authors such as Hans Christian Andersen and other writers to the Brocken region.

Even if Goethe and Heine's lyrical poems such as Goethe's stunningly evocative *Wayfarers' Night Song* ("Over all the hill tops is stillness..") are best known to English-speaking readers from the great German Lieder or classical song repertoire, the influence of that and their successors on the German speaking nations' deep love of forest, mountains and "Wanderung" – walking – remains a profound one, and, as we shall suggest, has also influenced much of what we think of as our uniquely British experience. Coleridge, in particular, was an avid reader of German literature and philosophy, and his own highly influential critical writing of later years reflected a powerful influence from our Continental neighbours, as indeed did the work of the English Romantics on many European writers and thinkers.

No single image better encapsulated the spirit of the early Romantic movement in Europe than the painting executed in 1818 by the great German Romantic painter Caspar David Friedrich (1774-1840) *Wanderer über dem Nebelmeer* (The Wanderer Across the Sea of Mist) which shows the painter/poet in the conventional riding boots and frock coat of his period standing with his walking stick on a rocky outcrop in the mountains, looking

Wanderer above a Sea of Mist – Caspar Friedrich.

across and into landscape of jagged, rocky outcrops appearing above the floating mist that half conceals and half reveals the hill tops and mountain ranges, which fade into a murky infinity of sky and remote distance.

This is exactly the kind of image you will still see on the cover and in the pages of walking, mountain and outdoor magazines in the 21st century, the awed individual – the *Rückenfigure* with whom we, the viewers, associate ourselves – staring into the picture, looking across at the vast, powerful and sublime beauty of nature. The painting is actually of a misty morning in the Sandsteingebirge, above the Elbe on the Czech border of East Germany, but it could equally well be Wordsworth's Cumberland. It's this feeling of the sublime, even moral power of mountain scenery, which has become deeply embedded in our own culture, reflecting our contemporary attitudes to mountains and fell landscape, even if the names William

Wordsworth or Caspar Friedrich mean nothing to us.

However, nowhere was the influence of the Lake Poets more profound than in the United States, where English Romantic ideas developed in a different and radical way through the philosophy of Transcendentalism. The core belief of the Transcendentalists such as Henry Thoreau and Ralph Waldo Emerson, both deeply influenced by Wordsworth of *The Prelude*, was the central importance to human thought of a spiritual state that 'transcends' physical and empirical understanding but can only be realised through an individual's intuition, rather than through the conventional doctrines of established religion or philosophy:

One impulse from a vernal wood
May teach you more of man,
Of moral evil and of good,
Than all the sages can.

In many ways Transcendentalism was a reaction against the sterility of much conventional scientific thought and religious orthodoxy of the time but also a very American way of following your own personal intuition and going back to the natural world, rediscovering the power of wilderness in yourself as well as in nature. The individual had to re-educate him or herself through practical experience and self-reliance, which included cultivating your own land, baking your own bread and of course walking.

David Henry Thoreau's (1817-62) celebrated *Walden* (1854) was about his rediscovery of the simple life in New England at Walden Pond, in Concord, Massachusetts in 1845, on land owned by his friend Emerson. The beautifully written, poetic account of his life there, and the home-spun philosophy that he evolved, is one of the great American classics, and arguably one of the most influential books of all time.

In an essay published in 1862 Thoreau describes the "art of walking" or even "sauntering" as a way of understanding one's environment and ultimately

Henry Thoreau.

John Muir.

one's own place within that environment. He describes how, within a short radius of where he lives, there are endless new worlds to be discovered on foot:

Two or three hours walking will carry me to as strange a country as I expect ever to see. A single farm-house which I had not seen before is sometimes as good as the dominions of the King of Dahomey. There is in fact a sort of harmony discoverable between the capabilities of the landscape within a circle of ten miles' radius, of the limits of an afternoon walk, and the three score years and ten of human life. It will never become quite familiar to you.... (Excursions)

Ralph Waldo Emerson (1803-1882), who had met both Wordsworth and Coleridge on his trip to Britain, became the leading philosopher of the Transcendentalist movement. A young Scottish immigrant, the author and naturalist John Muir (1838-1914), in his many long hikes across the mountains of America, actually met Emerson in Yosemite in 1871. Profoundly influenced by Transcendentalist philosophy, Muir became founder of the influential Sierra Club, the USA's leading conservation body, that continues to campaign for the protection of wilderness. Muir's campaigning led to the establishment and federal protection of Yosemite, one of the world's most celebrated National Parks, whilst his writing and philosophy was to become a huge inspiration for the conservation movement worldwide, leading to the creation of National Parks in Europe and eventually in Britain.

Victorian England's most influential artist, essayist and critic was John Ruskin 1819-1900. Like most later Romantics, Ruskin saw nature and the natural world as the greatest moral teacher of all, as interpreted by the painters – above all his beloved Turner who he ardently championed - and the architects of Renaissance Italy, especially Venice. He also championed Gothic architecture, reflecting, as he believed it did, natural forms of nature as epitomised in the crags and peaks of an Alpine landscape, and in the use of natural materials such as stone and even iron for building. Ruskin's work reflects a view that we unconsciously accept to this very day, that an experience of fine art and architecture, and especially of the natural world, of natural beauty, can in each and every person, even the "least thoughtful", elicit a response in which aesthetic pleasure is mingled with a sense of something more spiritual:

Whatever beauty there may result from effects of light on foreground objects, from the dew of the grass, the flash of the cascade, the glitter of the birch trunk, or the fair daylight hues of darker things (and joyfulness there is in all of them), there is yet a light which the eye invariably seeks with a deeper feeling of the beautiful, the light of the declining or breaking day, and the flakes of scarlet cloud burning like watch fires in the green sky of the horizon; a deeper feeling I say, not perhaps more acute, but having more of spiritual hope and longing, less of animal and present life, more manifest, invariably of those of more serious and determined mind (I use the word serious, not as opposed to cheerful but to trivial and volatile) but, I think, marked and unfailing even in those of the least thoughtful disposition.
(Modern Painters II Pt 3)

Beneath this complex syntax Ruskin offers a powerful moral justification both for a protected and fully accessible countryside, and for related environmental education. Ruskin's words underline the spiritual values – the "hope and longing" – that can emerge from an appreciation, at whatever level, of the aesthetic qualities of the natural world. This is a belief which has become one of the prime motivating forces of every campaign over the last century and a half for the protection of the countryside and to secure access for all to it. But its roots lie deep in the Romantic movement, and in Wordsworthian perceptions of the moral goodness of nature in particular.

Happily physical access to this countryside was now becoming much easier for ordinary people living in the new industrial cities. The coming of the railways in Britain, Europe and the United States from the 1840s onwards made access to even wilder areas of countryside possible for many more people. From this period onwards the first railway guidebooks appear, including the first detailed guidebooks specifically written for walkers using the new railways. Literacy was spreading rapidly with the growth of Board Schools from the 1870s onwards. New markets were being created for articles, pamphlets and books which would popularise walking as a way of discovering the countryside for a new generation.

Two writers who were to benefit from this growth in interest in exploring the countryside on foot were George Borrow and Robert Louis Stevenson. Borrow, born in Norwich in 1803, the son of an army officer, was a gifted but rebellious boy, soon consorting with local gypsies with whom he was roaming the local Norfolk countryside. He avoided a career in the law by becoming a writer. His (eventually) highly successful travel books included *Lavengro* (1851), *Romany Rye* (1857) and *Wild Wales* (1862).

Wild Wales gives a captivating picture of Wales in the mid 19th century. Borrow travelled on foot throughout his trip, with his possessions in a small leather satchel slung over his shoulder and carrying an umbrella. He generally stayed in country inns, taking a slightly unusual route through the Berwyn Mountains, Snowdonia, Ceredigion, the Black Mountains and even including the newly industrialised towns of Neath and Swansea on his itinerary. He mainly walked along the public roads where there was very little horse-drawn traffic, but also used by-roads and mountain tracks.

Borrow is the most entertaining of travelling

Ruskin and his study at Brantwood, Coniston 1882, painted by his secretary W G Collingwood.

George Borrow.

companions. Unlike the early Romantic writers, the people he meets are more important than the scenery, and Borrow's own personality perhaps even more than those he meets. Though he does indeed visit several well established tourist sights, including well described ascents of both Snowdon and Plynlimon, the real focus of the books are often very entertaining accounts of conversations in pubs, or on the road with Welsh people. He taught himself Welsh and could communicate remarkably well sometimes in a mixture of the two languages. Most of the narrative takes the form of dialogue. How much is accurately remembered and how much imagined is difficult to judge. But the descriptions of the walk itself have the ring of truth, for example when he crests a hill near Neath, in south Wales to discover the famous Neath Abbey surrounded by "grimly diabolical-looking buildings" and "accursed pandemonium" of what is now long vanished heavy industry. Or again he captures, with great accuracy, the sheer tedium of walking along a dreary moorland road through the mountains near Beddgelert in Snowdonia:

In about an hour I came to a wild moor; the moor extended for miles and miles. It was bounded on the east and south by immense hills and moels. On I walked at a round pace, the sun scorching me sore, along a dusty, hilly road, now up, now down. Nothing can be conveyed more cheerless than the scenery around. The ground on each side of the road was mossy and rushy – no houses – instead of them were peat stacks, here and there, standing in their blackness. Nothing living to be seen except a few miserable sheep, here and there, picking the wretched herbage or lying panting on the shady side of the peat clumps.

Robert Louis Stevenson's *Travels with a Donkey in the Cevennes* (1879) is another walking classic. Stevenson was the son of a Scottish lighthouse engineer and initially trained as an engineer and lawyer before becoming a full time writer, eventually writing the celebrated classic adventure stories *Treasure Island* and *Kidnapped*. In 1873 he suffered a nervous and physical breakdown and had to spend time in the warmer climate of France and the south of England to recuperate. As part of his recuperation he spent time in the village of Le Monastier in the Cevennes in 1878. In order to carry the luggage he needed for camping, he invented a unique form of "waterproof cart cloth" sleeping bag into which during the day time he could stuff all his necessary possessions. This was, of course, too heavy to carry, so he bought a small donkey, named Modestine, as a pack carrier. The book is a sparklingly written description of the journey, perhaps the first account to describe the joys of outdoor camping and sleeping under the stars.

Stevenson has the ability of a poet to capture the feel of a landscape in a few concise words:

Moor, heathery marsh, tracts or rock and pines, woods of birch all jewelled with the autumn yellow, here and there a few naked cottages and bleak fields – these were the characters of the country. Hill and valley followed valley and hill, the little green and stony cattle tracks wandered in and out of one another, split into three and four, died away in marshy hollows, and began again sporadically on hillside or at the border of a wood.

But the book also has its highly entertaining moments, such as the occasion when, in the centre of the village, Modestine's over-stuffed sleeping bag pack slipped from her back to underneath the belly, and RLS's efforts to right the load were witnessed by local villagers now helpless with laughter.

Robert Louis Stevenson.

By the later part of the 19th century, mountain climbing and walking guidebooks were being produced in their thousands for the newly emancipated lower middle and upper working class populations. Walking was attracting new markets.

One of England's greatest novelists and poets, Thomas Hardy (1840-1928), also wrote for this new market. Hardy was able to chronicle, over his long lifetime, in a series of remarkable novels, the rapid process of change in Britain from a largely agricultural to a largely industrial nation. His semi-fictional Wessex is filled, in almost anthropological detail, with descriptions of vanishing rural lifestyles, recorded during his early professional years as an architect and church restorer in Dorset. Most significant are the impacts on those lifestyles of the coming of the railways and of the new machine age on the farms.

But Thomas Hardy was also a passionate, energetic walker, who knew his local countryside intimately, and with a walker and countryman's eye for detail of the natural world. And above all is a deep sense of history in the landscape which can only come from a lifetime of careful understanding and observation. Many of his novels contain huge set-pieces of poetic description of the landscape which then, in a powerful way, permeate, just as in *Wuthering Heights*, the entire novel. Who can ever forget, for example, the description in *Return of the Native* (1878) of Egdon Heath in November with its feeling of menace, "the heathy, firzy, briary wilderness" which is "the enemy of civilisation":

To recline on a stump of thorn in the central valley of Egdon, between afternoon and night, as now, where the eye could reach nothing of the world outside the summits and shoulders of heathland which filled the whole circumference of its glance, and to know everything around and underneath had been from prehistoric times as unaltered as the stars overhead, gave ballast to the mind adrift on change and harassed by the irrepressible New. The great inviolate place had an ancient permanence which the sea cannot claim…
..
….*With the exception of an aged highway, and a still more aged barrow presently to be referred to – themselves almost crystallised to natural products by long continuance – even the trifling irregularities were not caused by pickaxe, plough or spade, but remained as the very finger-touches of the last geological change.*

This is a post-Darwinian, godless landscape, in which man's entire existence is a mere blink of an eyelid in geological time, where the human preoccupation with progress or "The New" is an irrelevance.

Hardy's novels explore this emergence of rural society into an often hostile, modern universe with in his greatest novels an almost Shakespearean intensity. Yet after the largely negative reception of the bleak *Jude the Obscure* in 1895 he wrote no more novels, but switched to poetry for the last 33 years of his life, producing an avalanche of powerful, often allusive verse which now make him among the greatest of English poets, dealing as they do in miniature and a compressed way with many of the themes of time, change, and ironic betrayal that run through the novels.

Thomas Hardy.

But in the poetry too, the recognisable insight of the walker remains, in the exactness of small details of description, the perception of the landscape and historic features within that landscape. His poetry is not easy to read. Archaic and even dialect words, awkward sentence structure, avoiding of surface polish create something deliberately earthy, rustic, which has seemingly grown out of the Dorset soil.

There are a few poems directly about walking, but even these have an ironic or sinister twist. *Paying Calls* starts happily enough:

I went by footpath and by stile
Beyond where bustle ends,
Stayed here a mile and there a mile
And called upon some friends.

It is only in the last verse of the poem that we understand that these friends are "by mound and stone and tree" in a rural graveyard and though he speaks to them of old times "ere days were dim" , "they spoke not to me".

A Wet Night opens with the poet walking vigorously through the heavy rain:

I pace along, the rain shafts riddling me,
Mile after mile out by the moorland way,
And upon the hill, and through the ewe-leaze gray
Into the lane, and round the corner tree;

Though his clothes are "mire-bestarred" and "clams" him, he reflects on the thousands of souls who have walked along this same way in such weather in years past. He has chosen to do so, as a rambler and leisure walker, perhaps out of perverse pleasure. He reflects on the fact that previous generations, who walked "in sturdy muteness" had no such choice.

A more celebrated poem, *Wessex Heights* (1896) has the narrator, who may or may not be the poet, seeking the summits of the Wessex hills as an escape from the pressures of life and the conflicts with others:

There are some heights in Wessex, shaped as if by a kindly hand
For thinking, dreaming, dying on, and at crisis when I stand
Say, on Ingpen Beacon eastwards, or on Wylls-Neck westwardly,
I seem where I was before my birth, and after death may be.

In the lowland and in the towns he claims to have no friends, only memories of "men with a wintry sneer and women with tart disparagings" or mysterious ghosts of unhappy events, but the hilltops paradoxically provide private places where the walker can be alone with his thoughts:

Where men have never cared to haunt, nor women have walked with me,
And ghosts then keep their distance: and I know some liberty.

One of Hardy's very last poems, and most moving, is simply called *Afterwards*. The poem predicts the poet's own death perhaps not far into the future:

When the present has latched its Postern behind my tremulous stay
at particular moment in the evening when the dewfall-hawk comes crossing the shades to alight upon the wind warped upland thorn .

The homely, earthy imagery and sharp detail hinges around that exactness of experience only shared by those who have been out in that environment, listening, watching, understanding:

And will any say when my bell of quittance is heard in the gloom,
And a crossing breeze cuts a pause in its outrollings,
Till they rise again, as they were a new bell's boom,
'He hears it not now but used to notice such things'?

No writer has more vividly established a sense of unique place in his writing than Hardy, nor the continuity of ancient times with the past, present, and future. This sense of place and time is a key aspect of much of what we now regard as environmental conservation, why particular landscapes are as they are, and why they should be protected and conserved, as a part of that continuity of human experience we all need for our psychological health and survival, something Hardy, intuitively, understood so well.

Another remarkable late Victorian walker-writer was the novelist George Gissing (1857-1903) whose premature death from emphysema was ironically hastened when he caught a chill when out on a winter walk. His fine novel of female emancipation and independence, *Odd Women* (1873), has a heroine, Rhoda Nunn who is taken by her admirer on a romantic assignation which includes a trip along the narrow gauge tourist railway through Eskdale in the Lake District. From the little train's then terminus station at Boot, the rambler-lovers head off up the path towards Wasdale:

A mountain torrent roared by the wayside. And the course they had marked upon the map showed that they must follow this stream for some miles up to the tarn

Boot station, the original terminus of the narrow gauge Ravenglass & Eskdale Railway. around 1905. The line features in the 1894 novel, Odd Women, by George Gissing, when his heroine Rhoda makes a walking trip into the Lake District.

where it originated. Houses, human beings, and even trodden paths they soon left behind, coming out on a vast moorland, with hill summits near and far. Scawfell they could not hope to ascend; with the walk that lay before them it was enough to make a way over one of his huge shoulders.

George Gissing.

Sadly the relationship does not work out in the way Rhoda hopes – her young man, in spite of him bringing chicken sandwiches and a flask of wine with "a wine glass which was for Rhoda's use" in his shoulder bag, a day or so after their ramble in the hills, it all ends with tears and a parting, on a rainy morning, in Seascale station.

But few writers have ever more evocatively captured the magic of a country walk than Gissing in his rather strange collection of autobiographical essays, *The Private Papers of Henry Ryecoft* (1903), in which he gives a series of brief, yet vivid, thumb-nail sketches of special parts of the countryside where he has enjoyed favourite walks. These include Suffolk, Gloucestershire, the Cotswolds, the South Downs, the Sussex Weald Cambridgeshire and the Yorkshire Dales – the magic of climbing out of a valley towards high moorland as in his evocative description of a summer day's walk in Wensleydale:

I am in Wensleydale, climbing from the rocky river that leaps amid broad pastures up to the rolling moor. Up and up, till my feet brush through heather, and the grouse whirrs away before me. Under a glowing sky of summer, this air of the uplands has a still life which spurs to movement, which makes the heart bound. The dale is hidden; I see only the brown and purple wilderness, cutting against the blue with great round shoulders, and far away to the west, an horizon of sombre heights....

Edward Thomas.

One of the finest 20th century poets and essayists who was also a passionate walker was Edward Thomas (1878-1917), tragically killed at the battle of Arras in the final weeks of the First World War. Though born in London, Thomas' poems totally reflect the Welsh and the Gloucestershire countryside where he spent his adult years. His work reveals a passion for rambling in the countryside, a resultant knowledge of the natural world and country people, and of footpaths. For example writing about rural Oxfordshire, (the neighbouring county to Gloucestershire), he describes a familiar walk with an almost sensual delight of the visual beauty, sounds and even evocative scents experienced when out leisure walking:

The Oxford county is rich in footpaths, as anyone will know that goes the round from Folly Bridge through South Hinksey to the 'Fox' at Boar's Hill (where the scent of wallflowers and hawthorn comes in through the window with the sound of the rain and the nightingale); and then away, skirting Wooton and Cumnor, past the 'Bear' (with its cool flagged room looking on a field of gold, and Cumnor church among the elms) and back over the Hurst, where he turns, under seven firs, to ponder the long, alluring view towards Stanton Harcourt and Bablock Hythe. He may take that walk many times, or wish to take it, and yet never touch the same footpaths; and never be sure of the last patch of bluebell and furze, haunted by linnet and whinchat; the newly harrowed field, where the stones shine like ivory after rain; the green lane where the beech leaves lie in February, and rise out of the snow, untouched by it in polished amber; the orchard, where grass is gloomy in April with the shadow of bright cherry flowers.

(Oxford)

He also wrote one of the first guidebooks to any long distance route, the Icknield Way, well before long distance walking of such a route became fashionable in Britain. But it is above all his beautiful, suggestive poems which magically recreate the intimacy of a walker's countryside that is the essential Edward Thomas. Typical is the poem called simply *The Path*, which describes a footpath running alongside the parapet of a road that is used by children to enjoy the view below the road:

The path, winding like silver, trickles on,
Bordered, and even invaded by thinnest moss
That tries to cover roots and crumbling chalk
With gold, olive, emerald, but in vain.
The children wear it. They have flattened the bank
On top, and silvered it between the moss
With the current of their feet, year after year.

– but the path goes nowhere and, a typical Thomas touch, suddenly ends, mysteriously, in the wood.

Of more recent writers, the Cumbria poet Norman Nicholson (1914-1987) not only produced perhaps the best guidebooks to the Lake District since Wordsworth, but some of the finest poetry about the Lakeland hills and their geological structures. These do not just describe the tourist landscapes but the industrial fringes of Workington, Cleator Moor and above all his native Millom, with its old ironworks and industrial communities. His poems have a directness, a linguistic freshness, which like Wordsworth at his youthful best, attempts to get back to the strong vowels and rhythms of local speech. His poem *Scarth Gap, Buttermere*, describes with accuracy a celebrated Lakeland pass "like a pencil drawn diagonally across the slate":

The pass is known, defined and understood
Not by the eyes but by the feet,
The feet of men and sheep that tread it: the young
Teacher from Cleator Moor, pushing a bike
With a burnish of poetry on the rims
The girl who is soon to bear a foreigner's child:
The lad who leaves the pit shafts of Solway
To grope for a brighter fire than coal.

This is the democratisation of the Lakeland fells in the 20th century, the hills are now accessible to everyone. The walkers head for the queue of hills – High Stile and Mellbreak, Robinson, Grassmoor and Hobcarton Fell. But it ends with a Hardyesque touch:

A track that the wild herdwicks will still tread
Long after the makers of tracks are dead.

If Nicholson was inevitably influenced by that "oldish man with a nose like a pony's nose" as he characterised Wordsworth, perhaps the influence is less expected in another more celebrated 20th century poet, Ted Hughes (1930-1998). Hughes' early work in particular is imbued with a strong sense of landscape and place, especially his native Calderdale, but above all he deals with the raw power, even violence of nature. Nature in Hughes is far less benign than Wordsworth's.

His poem *The Horses* describes a pre-dawn walk climbing out of a Pennine valley towards a group of ten "megalith-still" horses high on the hillside. He listens a few moments in the silence as the morning sun slowly erupts above the moorland horizon ahead and suddenly lights up the scene, before he continues to climb, past the horses, their "hung heads patient as the horizons".

For Hughes, it is one of those pivotal Wordsworthian "spots of time" where he hopes that:

In the din of the crowded streets, going among the years, the faces,
May I still meet my memory in so lonely a place
Between the streams and the red clouds, hearing curlews,
Hearing the horizons endure.

It is also a description that perfectly captures the magic of a dawn walk, anywhere, but especially in an upland landscape such as the Pennines, but in this case the intensity of the experience recreates that of the early Romantics.

In the later 20th and early 21st centuries, if there has been less major work by leading poets, novelists or essayists about walking in the countryside, it is partly perhaps because these themes have been so well explored. It is difficult simply to repeat what greater writers have already done so vividly and well. But it may also be that walking as an expression of feeling about the environment or as a philosophical statement is no longer perceived as relevant to a younger generation. You are more likely to read a reference in contemporary verse to a poet driving his car over the moors than walking across them. Maybe poets don't walk or walkers don't write poetry, or more likely that with the shades of so many greater writers behind you, this is a topic you don't feel really able to tackle.

There may be another reason too. There is now a huge avalanche of outdoor writing, some of it very fine, with literally thousands of superbly written and illustrated walking and climbing guidebooks. Walking books now cover every corner of Britain in meticulous detail. Climbing books in particular have developed into a genre of their own, and if you are a brilliant climber of the Joe Simpson or Chris Bonington calibre and can also take superb photographs and write well, or you are an explorer like Fiennes or Fogle, then your descriptions of the world's mountain landscapes, arctic snows and wilder seas, based on first-hand experience, are likely to be a good deal more convincing than that of the more dilettante poet. Writing about wilderness, like so many other themes, is now a specialist area.

But such more specialised accounts are different from the gentler art of walking through Britain's countryside that this book is primarily about. An exception perhaps is Alfred Wainwright, who in a generation has moved from being regarded as a specialist writer and illustrator for Lakeland climbers and fell walkers, to an author who has had a profound influence on leisure walking in Britain, especially long distance walking as we shall see in a later section of this book.

Ultimately the Romantic Revolution achieved a profound shift in taste and created ideas which still influence our thoughts and beliefs about walking and the countryside as well as our leisure activities. Poets were inspired by walking and poetry inspired walkers. In particular the Romantic and post Romantic writers created an ideology in which leisure walking was perceived to be a way of escaping from the artificiality of modern industrial civilisation to establish a new, personal relationship with the natural world. In the two centuries or so since the publication of Wordsworth's and Coleridge's *Lyrical Ballads*, in a world threatened by the excesses of industrial civilisation, over-consumption and alienation from the natural world, those ideas have never been more relevant.

3. WALKING AND PROTEST – THE OUTDOOR MOVEMENT

We ramblers, after a hard week's work in smoky towns and cities, go out rambling for relaxation, a breath of fresh air, a little sunshine. But what we find when we go out, that the finest rambling country is closed to us, just because certain individuals wish to shoot for about ten days a year – Benny Rothman

Much of the countryside of modern Britain was largely shaped by a series of Enclosure Acts which transformed the landscape in the last decades of the 18th and first decades of the 19th century. The process of Enclosure, parish by parish, of the medieval open commons and strip fields created the familiar patchwork of small fields of pasture or arable crops, behind carefully maintained hedges, fences and dry stone walls that we now regard as typical English or Welsh "countryside". But this landscape is a purely artificial one, and was largely created over a relatively brief period of around 60 years.

The process was a necessary part of what economic historians refer to as the Agrarian Revolution to feed Britain's growing population and create new prosperity by massively increasing the efficiency of farming. By 1800 the more intensively farmed agricultural land of England was feeding half as many people again as it had in 1750, and corn production had increased by 43% during the century as many areas of "waste" or rough grazing were brought into production. This process continued through the first half of the 19th century. Animal husbandry benefited from well drained, fertile pastures compared with the scrub and rough grass of open commons, and new varieties of crops flourished in well manured arable fields.

A gradual process of amalgamation of many small, uneconomic post-Enclosure farms into ever larger land holdings created a new class of prosperous farmer-landlords. In the process it created new wealth which was to provide much of the venture capital to be invested in Britain's rapidly growing international trade and industrialisation. It also clarified land ownership rights, allowing larger land and estate owners to mine the rich seams of coal on their land, quarry the building stone, build the new roads, canals and eventually railways required to transform Britain into the world's first industrial superpower.

But there was a terrible human price to pay. Millions of poorer rural cottagers, small farmers and labourers lost the right to graze their pig or cow on the open land, and with it a vital source of supplementary income and support.

John Clare, from a family of poor Northamptonshire cottagers, was one of the few writers to experience, at first hand, what this meant, which included a loss of freedom to walk freely over the common and heathland, "free as the lark" rather than being confined to roads within an enclosed landscape with:

Fence meeting fence in owner's little bounds
Of field and meadow, large as garden grounds,
In little parcels little minds to please,
With men and flocks imprisoned, ill at ease.

But it was more than just the physical changes, but loss of small but important rights, not just as grazing rights, but rights of "turbary" – the right to cut peat, "estovers" – fallen twigs or branches of wood for kindling or building – or "pannage" – the right to allow your pigs to eat acorns in a woodland. This brought many family incomes down to below even modest subsistence levels, and according to Clare "left the poor a slave".

The distress was palpable. Pauperism was

common, with poor law rates dramatically increased as rural families literally faced near starvation and had to be fed on the parish rate.

As the historian Roy Porter writes:

Within sixty or seventy years of enclosure, practically all the smaller owner-occupiers had disappeared. The lower orders had lost all ownership of the means of rural production and had become rural labourers or framework knitters.

The dispossessed rural poor survived by migrating in their tens of thousands and eventually millions from Britain's countryside into the rapidly expanding cities of London, Bristol, Birmingham, Staffordshire, Manchester, South Wales, Southern Scotland and the West Riding of Yorkshire. Industrial Britain required huge numbers of workers to man the new coal mines, flax, cotton and wool mills, foundries, factories, shipyards that were being built and expanded at unprecedented speed. It was not only rural England but Wales, Scotland and Ireland which provided vast numbers of migrant workers to fuel the rapid process of industrialisation. As well as Rural Enclosure, the inward migration to the industrial towns of Britain and outward migration to the colonies were accelerated by two of the darkest episodes of British history – the barbaric Highland Clearances of the late 18th and early 19th centuries for the benefit of often absentee Scottish landowners, and the Irish Potato Famine, where millions were literally left to starve to death after the disastrous failure of the Irish potato crop. These migrant workers formed the basis of a new proletariat, an ill-educated, impoverished working class, prepared to take any work for low wages.

Provision for anything more than the most basic physical needs of the new workforce was largely ignored by the new factory, mill and mine owners. Housed in inadequate, cramped cottages or cellared tenements close to the factories they served, with poor or non-existent sanitation facilities, these jerry-built properties created the growing slums of London, Manchester, Liverpool, Leeds, Sheffield, Birmingham and Glasgow. They created a world about which polite society knew nor cared little or nothing.

It was left to a young 24 year old German, the son of a textile manufacturer from Berlin, Friedrich Engels, to describe the squalor to a wider audience. As the Manchester Agent of his father's business, Engels saw for himself the often appalling, inhuman and insanitary conditions of the slums, hotbeds of cholera and typhoid, in which working families were thrust. His classic study *Condition of the Working Class in England* (1844) described graphically the human degradation into which people lived in both London and Manchester. He reports on a typical slum area by the River Medlock, close to Oxford Road:

The cottages are old, dirty, and of the smallest sort, the streets uneven, fallen into ruts and in part without drains or pavement; masses of refuse, offal and sickening filth lie among standing pools in all directions; the atmosphere is poisoned by the effluvia from these, and laden and dark by the smoke of a dozen chimneys. A horde of ragged women and children swam about here, as filthy as the swine that thrive upon the garbage heaps and in the puddles....

The novelist and biographer Elizabeth Gaskell, who was also the wife of a Unitarian Minister in Central Manchester, in her novel *Mary Barton* (1848) also graphically describes conditions in a central Manchester slum street, close to what is now Manchester Piccadilly Station, a sight which, as the wife of a local Minister visiting the distressed, must have been all too familiar to her:

It was unpaved; and down the middle a gutter forced its way, ever now and then forming pools in the holes with which the street abounded. Never was the Old Edinburgh cry of "Gardez L'eau" more necessary than in this street. As they passed, women from their doors tossed household slops of every description into the gutter, they ran into the next pool which overflowed and stagnated. Heaps of ashes were the stepping stones, on which the passer-by, who cared in the least for cleanliness, took care not to put his foot.

Elizabeth Gaskell.

Slum conditions became commonplace in the early nineteenth century. This photograph depicts the Quarry Hill district of Leeds, but could have been taken in almost any industrial city.

Yet even in such a crowded and polluted city, there were still a few surviving green spaces, not yet built on, on the edge of the built-up areas, and the novel opens with a description of the footpath which leads over a stile through Green Heys Fields on the outskirts of town, where every Sunday or holiday people would be drawn out of the smoke polluted city streets to sit, stroll, meet friends or go courting. It was a place where, in Mrs Gaskell's words, the townsfolk cut off from the countryside could see the country business of haymaking, ploughing which are such "pleasant mysteries for townspeople to watch".

Given the appalling conditions suffered by so many people it was perhaps astonishing that open revolt and revolution did not occur, though it came close, with constant protest meetings, ad-hoc riots and civil disturbances, a frequent occurrence in many regions of Britain. There were also numerous not always well organised protest movements such as the Luddites, hand loom weavers who took the law into their own heads by smashing the new mechanised looms in mills in Yorkshire and Lancashire, Chartists who campaigned for electoral reform, and even embryonic Communists whose naïve beliefs in common ownership were fuelled by French idealists such as Rousseau and Babeuf. The reaction of the horrified authorities to such developments was to take ever more repressive and panic measures, with armed troops barracked within or close to many of the new industrial towns. A flash point occurred at St Peter's Fields in Manchester in August 1819 when a peaceful crowd estimated to be between 60,000 to 80,000 strong met to demand electoral reform. However they were faced with an ill-judged cavalry charge by the Manchester & Salford Yeomanry, brought in to support the issuing of a warrant to arrest the leading orator Henry Hunt and some of his colleagues. The charge left 15 people dead and between 400 and 700 wounded, and was forever known as the Peterloo Massacre.

Whilst the immediate result of the Peterloo Massacre was even more repressive measures by the authorities, it ignited an awareness among liberal thinkers, not just in Manchester but further afield. One result was the founding of the *Manchester Guardian* newspaper – now *The Guardian* – and a strengthening of the resolve of many liberal minded individuals to change what had become, for the less fortunate social classes, a brutalised and inhumane society.

Much of the profoundest transformation of life in Britain, which occurred in the middle and later Victorian era, came about as a result of the emergence of a newly energised political and progressive minded elite. Without the constant reforms and civic improvements achieved in many areas of life over the next few decades, the economic, political and social pressures may well have led, as they did in other European countries, to more violent forms of revolution. But the reformers got their way. New sewerage systems, clean water, paved streets, better transport, better housing, better education, new hospitals, schools, museums and art galleries, and even public parks enabled destructive forces to be channelled into more worthwhile causes.

However, the wider countryside beyond the edge of the town was, for most second or third generation town dwellers, somewhere so unknown and mysterious. It could have been on the other side of the world, even though distant folk memory of a rural past remained in a collective memory, in folk lore, nursery rhymes and metaphor.

But even as early as 1833, a year after the famous Reform Act to improve Parliamentary representation, a House of Commons Select Committee was established "to consider the best means of securing open spaces in the vicinity of populous towns as public walks and places of exercise, calculated to promote the health and comfort of inhabitants".

One of the people giving evidence to the Committee was one Dr James Phillips Kay of Manchester (1804-1877) (who was later to change his name to Kay-Shuttleworth), the doctor and social reformer, who had just dealt with the effects of the terrible cholera epidemic in the town during the previous year. He wrote:

Healthful exercise in the open air is seldom or never taken by the artisans of this town, and their health suffers considerably from this deprivation. The reason of this state of the people is that all scenes of interest are remote from the town, and the walks that can be enjoyed by the poor are chiefly the turnpike roads, alternately dusty or muddy. Were parks provided, recreation would be taken with avidity, and one of the first results would be better use of the Sunday, and a substitution of innocent amusements at all other time for the debasing pleasures now in vogue.

Kay-Shuttleworth was perhaps the first person of any authority to articulate the link between walking and health, and the need to secure green spaces in which healthful walking could take place. Significantly the Commission was to recommend the creation of more "public walks and open spaces" within or close to large towns and even a Thames-side walk in London where people could "walk out with decent comfort with their families". As we see in Chapter 6, this was to set in motion campaigns to develop and create public parks and open space in towns and cities throughout Britain.

But by the mid 19th century, another means of accessing the countryside from towns had been created and was being rapidly developed – the steam railway.

Britain's railway network became a major instrument of both economic and social change. It was also a means to reconnect the urban millions with their lost rural past. By the 1860s and '70s most rural areas had their branch railways, to carry both freight and passengers, connecting with the main lines, with country stations to serve rural communities. But the new network was equally available for townspeople to go out into the countryside, and it made commercial sense for the railway companies to attract passengers to fill their trains in both directions.

By the 1840s, railway companies had even Wordsworth's beloved Lake District in their sights. The once radical, visionary poet of utopian ideals was now a High Tory Pillar of the Establishment (and writer of unreadable doggerel verse) who was horrified by the idea of the proletariat coming even to the edge of the Lake District by train:

'Is there no nook of English ground secure
From rash assault?'

he asks in a sonnet 1844, before asking his readers to "protest against the wrong" – though later plans to extend the railway to Ambleside and connect to Keswick through the heart of the Lake District via Grasmere and Thirlmere with a tunnel under Dunmail Raise suggest he may have had a point.

Ironically in the 1970s, conservationists were protesting strongly against the proposed closure of Wordsworth's hated Windermere branch railway, which mercifully survives and is now a very well used sustainable method of travelling to the Lake District National Park.

Once the railway lines were built railway

Early steam-hauled trains played a vital role in taking walkers into the countryside. Typical late-Victorian train at Kents Bank station. The service is on its way to Windermere, already a favoured base for those with a passion for the outdoors.

Windermere from Orrest Head. Lithograph by James Pyne (1800-1870). One of 25 views that he completed for inclusion in a book *The English Lake District* published in 1853. Several figures are depicted on top of this famous viewpoint. The scene had then recently changed with completion in 1847 of the Kendal & Windermere Railway – despite opposition from Wordsworth. A train can be seen on the left-hand side of the illustration.

companies were quick to seize the opportunity to market leisure trips into the countryside using their new services. Railway excursions, pioneered by Thomas Cook in the 1840s but later by the railway companies themselves, were a common way of filling special trains from the urban centres to seaside resorts, and also to popular areas of countryside, eventually becoming special ramblers' excursion trains on summer Sundays, with dedicated guided walks provided from the trains, a facility which continued right until the 1970s.

Railway guidebooks also began to appear, again both sponsored by the railway companies but also by private publishers and authors, seeing a new opportunity in the market, often with the support and help of the railways themselves. As early as 1853, the remarkable Yorkshire geologist John Phillips produced what might be one of the first ever guides to walking from a railway station when in *Excursions in Yorkshire by the North Eastern Railway* he complains about a lack of a horse bus from Richmond Station (in North Yorkshire), but recommends a walk from Richmond into Swaledale to enjoy its beauties, taking a careful look, of course, at local geology as you do.

Phillips was an interesting figure. Nephew of the pioneering field geologist and canal engineer William "Strata" Smith, he was also a close friend of the great geologist Professor Adam Sedgwick, teacher of and later opponent of Charles Darwin. Sedgwick (1785-1874) born in Dentdale in the Yorkshire Dales close to the Lakes, was a regular

John Phillips
1800 - 1874.

fell-walking companion of Wordsworth, and contributed for his friend a series of fine geological "Letters" dedicated to his rambling companion on the geology of the Lake District. These were published as appendices to various editions of Wordsworth's own much reprinted *Guide to the Lakes.*

Both Sedgwick and Phillips (who went on to found the British Association for the Advancement of Science) were inspiring writers and lecturers who did much to educate increasing numbers of women as well as men about the natural beauty and scientific interest of the countryside. They were pioneers of what might now be described as the adult education movement, linked as their lectures and classes were to the new Mechanics' Institutes, Literary and Philosophical Societies and new technical colleges being established in towns and cities. Men and women walked literally scores of miles to listen to Sedgwick's lectures in Kendal and Cambridge and Phillips in York on geology, palaeontology and the creation of the British landscape. Both men constantly urged their audiences to get out into the countryside to see, discover, explore for themselves. Their students were the teachers, clergymen, doctors, lawyers, the new generation of an emerging, better educated professional class who were to form the background of the outdoor, amenity and walking movement.

These were the people ready and willing to buy new guidebooks soon rolling off the presses. Karl Baedeker established his travel book company in 1827 just before the railway boom, but was soon producing railway-based guidebooks to the whole of Europe that were the constant companions of Victorian and Edwardian British travelling abroad. But there were many British equivalents using what, by later Victorian times, was an incredibly extensive network of local rural lines.

By the 1870s, Edward Stanford of Charing Cross, for example, was producing his popular railway-based "Tourists' Guides" to various counties of England. Typical was the guide to the East and North Ridings of Yorkshire by G. Phillips Beavan which had, by 1887, gone into four editions. This is entirely based on exploring the area by the North Eastern Railway's network with detailed descriptions of the train journey along numerous, now long vanished, rural branch lines and the unusual "sights" and attractions close to stations. But walks were also included that could be accessed from local stations, for example the walk to the summit of a celebrated local viewpoint in the North York Moors, Roseberry Topping, from Guisborough Station. The reader is duly advised to walk along the Middlesbrough road before:

– turning l. beneath the railway. Then pass close to Hutton Hall, near which the path emerges on the moors. Roseberry Topping (topping, eminence) is a lias peak, 1067 feet, with a sandstone capping; and although no great height, it stands so isolated at the end of a mountain ridge, that the views are wonderfully fine, extending S. over the Cleveland Moors.....

This is a book written for an educated, knowledgeable audience. It is not surprising therefore to find the first formally organised walking groups or clubs being initiated and inspired by this same educated elite, steeped in the culture of the Romantic poets, the American Transcendentalists, and contemporary writers such as Hardy, Stevenson and George Borrow, as well as the geologists and naturalists such as Adam Sedgwick, Philip Henslow, John Phillips and in later years Darwin's great protagonist Thomas Huxley.

Given the nature of Victorian society, predictably Cambridge University led the way in England. The distinguished editor, writer and mountaineer Sir Leslie Stephen (founder editor of the Dictionary of National Biography but perhaps even better known as the father of Virginia Woolf and Vanessa Bell) was conqueror of several Alpine peaks, and President of the Alpine Club – another organisation dominated by Englishmen – between 1865 and 1868. In 1879, Stephen, a formidable walker, organised a series of regular walks into the local countryside of Cambridgeshire and eventually further afield. These were supported by his students and colleagues at the University, who were out most weekends and called themselves, with more than a touch of irony (as most were fairly well-heeled), The Sunday Tramps.

The group soon had around 60 members, many of them already or soon to become distinguished writers, essayists, philosophers, economists, civil servants who met for regular walks in the Cambridge area, using the local rail network from Cambridge or London.

But it wasn't just in Cambridge that walking was being promoted for health and for environmental education. A parallel walking club, in London, was the Forest Rambling Club. The Club was formed in 1884 and claims to be England's oldest walking club still in existence (and commendably the Club still bases all its walks around local rail transport). The Club's charmingly worded objective is "carrying out short rambles to places tending to helpful and instructive recreation and antiquarian interest". In 1885 they were followed by the still flourishing Polytechnic Rambling Club.

The Forest Rambling Club also owes its origin to a specific environmental campaign - to support the City of London Corporation in their work to conserve Epping Forest, which they had recently acquired after a major political battle some years earlier.

The saving of Epping Forest was the direct result of brilliant campaigning by Britain's oldest amenity organisation, the Commons Preservation Society which started life as a protest movement. The General Inclosure Act of 1845 was intended to provide protection for the remaining areas of open land or common not yet enclosed within five miles of any town of 10,000 or more inhabitants. The hope was to see such remaining open land used either for allotment gardens or for recreation. But the Act was increasingly ignored or subverted by powerful financial interests and property developers, especially in the English lowlands close to the larger cities such as London, where there was huge incentive to use open land for housing development. Surviving areas of unenclosed common land, village green and even precious fragments of former Royal Forest continued to be enclosed and developed during the 1850s and '60s.

In 1865 an energetic Liberal MP, George Shaw-Lefèvre, and a group of his friends formed the Commons Preservation Society to encourage the formation of local committees to fight the enclosure of these remaining commons. Though most battles took place in law courts, on a famous occasion in 1866 the Society took the law into its own hands when at Berkhamsted, Hertfordshire, local hero Augustus Smith MP, with the support of the Commons Preservation Society, hired a team of East End navvies. Armed with crowbars, they were brought out by special train at night in what became known as the Battle of Berkhamsted Common to tear down five feet high post and metal railings erected by Lord Brownlow's Trustees. Berkhamsted Common remains open to the public to this day.

Amongst early backers of the Society were Thomas Hughes, best known as author of Tom Brown's Schooldays, and the eminent philosopher John Stuart Mill. The Society fought a protracted battle through the courts and the corridors of political power over a decade and a half to save the remains of the former Royal Forest of Epping on the fringe of a rapidly expanding London from enclosure and development, and secure its future as a publicly-owned open space. When victory was finally secured in 1882, Queen Victoria herself rode through the Forest in an open carriage with two of

Roseberry Topping, which featured in early railway guidebooks. (Natural England – Mike Kipling)

her daughters to dedicate Epping Forest "to the use and enjoyment of the public for all time".

But preservation of a common did not necessarily mean access to that common, even though the admirable Law of Property Act of 1925 eventually granted public access on foot to all urban commons in England and Wales (that is common land situated in a former Urban District Council area).

One of the regular members of Leslie Stephen's Sunday Tramps was George Trevelyan, the eminent historian and essayist, who was to become a major champion of walking in the countryside, and the first President, in 1930, of the Youth Hostels Association. Trevelyan's celebrated essay *Walking*, first published in 1913, compared the freedom of walking in the Italian Apennines with England:

It is a land of hills and mountains, unenclosed, open in all directions to the wanderer at will, unlike some British mountain game-preserves. And even in the plains, the peasant, unlike some south-English farmers, never orders you off his ground, not even out of his olive grove or vineyard.

For Victorian and Edwardian ramblers, even in an enclosed, lowland landscape, road walking along country roads was a pleasurable and acceptable experience, as such traffic as there was, at least until the early 20th century, was horse drawn and

George Trevelyan.

Start of the walking match at Worth Village Gala, near Keighley, about 1905. This era has been referred to as 'the height of walking fever'.

relatively slow moving. Many country lanes away from the towns and the main turnpike roads were little more than unsurfaced, rutted sandy or stony tracks, dusty in summer and muddy in winter, with little traffic apart from the occasional horse rider or carrier's cart.

Nevertheless there was concern to protect footpaths and bridleways. Only a modest percentage of these had survived the process of Enclosure which should have safeguarded their existence, their legal existence recorded and mapped in Enclosure Awards, with stiles and gates erected where they crossed walls. But not only were many footpaths ignored during the process of Enclosure, even some ancient roads which had been used by horse and cart disappeared.

The earliest known organisation created purely to protect footpaths was the Association for the Protection of Ancient Footpaths in the Vicinity of York established in 1824. It was shortly followed by the Manchester Association for the Preservation of Ancient footpaths in 1826, formed to prevent the closure of footpaths in the Flixton area west of the city. This Association was a precursor of the Peak and Northern Footpath Society, founded in 1894.

The Peak and Northern's finest hour perhaps came when after years of campaigning, in 1896 it secured "for ever" the Snake Path, a popular walkers' route over Kinder Scout in the Derbyshire Peak District between Hayfield and the Snake Inn, which was to be marked by the Society's handsome metal signs (some of which still survive) and a new bridge that was built over Lady Brook. Further victories were secured when in 1912, and finally in

Protest meeting at the summit of Latrigg, near Keswick, October 1973. The abortive protests by about a thousand people were against the building of the A66 through northern Lakeland. In 1887 some two thousand people walked up Latrigg along disputed paths, thus creating a right of walk from Keswick to Skiddaw.

1928, it kept open the famous Doctor's Gate Path near Glossop.

The Peak and Northern is still one of the leading champions of public rights of way in the Peak District and North West of England. The Society still organises regular public walks to assert and protect rights of way.

But even visitors to the Lake District whether by carriage or the newly built railway faced problems. The Highways Act of 1835 had made the "wilful obstruction" of public rights of way an offence, but you had to prove there was a right of way there in the first place, and sometimes that could be extremely difficult to establish. Often the only redress was to literally smash down the obstruction and force your way through. William Wordsworth himself no less had to help to tear down a wall obstructing an old green road (accompanied by two senior judges) between Ullswater and Lowther Castle.

A local footpath protection society, the Keswick & District Footpath Preservation Association, founded in the 1850s soon after Wordsworth's death in order to keep alive his interest in retaining ancient footpaths, found itself involved in several major battles to retain locals paths from closure as new owners in particular resented the increasing number of visitors crossing their property on foot. This included two famous cases of the 1880s – a path along the shores of Derwentwater and to the popular summit of Latrigg above Keswick. In the case of Latrigg a series of protest walks took place, including the final one on 1 October 1887 when 2,000 people walked behind local Radical MP Samuel Plimsoll. This included eleven men carrying crowbars, pickaxes and spades, with everyone singing Rule Britannia as they reached the summit. Following further battles in the courts, a compromise solution was reached and public access to the summit of Latrigg was secured for ever.

Not all battles to safeguard long established footpaths were equally successful. When in summer 1896 a wealthy industrialist and landowner, Colonel Ainsworth decided to close a popular track, Coalpit Lane, over Winter Hill, in the West Pennines moors near Bolton, Lancashire, to protect his grouse moors, local activists organised a series of protest walks. On Sunday

September 6th over 10,000 people took part in a ramble to reclaim the lane, an event eclipsed by an even greater procession of 12,000 a few days later. There was even a song with words written in dialect by local poet "Teddy Ashton" to commemorate the occasion:

Will Yo Come o' Sunday Mornin'
For a Walk o're Winter Hill,
Ten thousand went last Sunday
But there's room for thousands still.

Despite this huge show of public support, injunctions were served on the ten ringleaders "to restrain them from trespassing". Despite a huge amount of evidence to support the existence of an ancient right of way, the judgement went against the protesters and they were heavily fined. The Battle of Winter Hill was lost; Coalpit Lane remained closed and the moors above Bolton remained forbidden to the people of Bolton for generations.

In 1884 a National Footpaths Society was established which soon had a membership of several hundred. Within a year of its formation 124 cases of "interference" with public footpaths were being dealt with. In 1899 the NFS was incorporated into the Commons Protection Society which from 1910 became known as the Commons, Open Spaces and Footpaths Preservation Society – and is now simply The Open Spaces Society. The Society continues to protect Britain's surviving open spaces, even including areas of now properly registered common land and village greens from the depravations of private developers and government agencies. It remains one of Britain's leading conservation groups, campaigning for the interests both of local communities (with many Parish and Community Councils as members) and walkers, protecting local footpaths and precious areas of green space in both town and countryside, as true guardians of an increasingly vital public heritage.

Access to the countryside and safeguarding of public rights of way remains inexorably linked to the protection of that countryside, the peaceful enjoyment of which was the purpose of securing that access on foot. These are the twin, closely intertwined great campaigning themes that have dominated the outdoor and countryside movement

A group of walkers on a Lake District Fell. From left to right are Benny Horne, a solicitor to the National Trust; Robert Hunter; his daughter Winnie Hunter; and Canon Hardwicke Rawnsley, Vicar of Crosthwaite. Hunter and Rawnsley were leading lights in forming the Lake District Defence Society and in defeating proposals in the 1880s for railways through Borrowdale and Ennerdale. Along with Dame Octavia Hill, they went on to form the National Trust in 1894.

Above: Beatrix Potter, her father Rupert Potter and Canon Rawnsley.
Left: Octavia Hill.

over the last century and a half. They fuelled on-going battles for ever more effective legislation and protection of these priceless national assets throughout the late 19th and during the entire 20th century. They will doubtless continue to do so throughout the present century.

Protection of the countryside and open spaces for freedom to walk were also to come together through the formation of one of Britain's great institutions – the National Trust. In its formative years it owed much to the work of three great radical figures – Robert (Bob) Hunter (1844-1913), a keen walker and lawyer who was legal Adviser to the Post Office and Honorary Solicitor to the Commons Preservation Society; Octavia Hill (1838-1912), the remarkable campaigner for facilities for the poor, including social housing; and the hyper-energetic Lakeland clergyman and campaigner Hardwicke Rawnsley (1851-1920), perhaps better known as Canon Rawnsley.

Hunter, Hill and Rawnsley shared a passion not only for protecting the countryside, but encouraging the less fortunate to experience and share that enjoyment.

Octavia Hill in particular developed the notion, which still has a powerful resonance in the 21st century, that access to the countryside is essential to the well-being of all people living and working in the urban environment. She helped secure the pioneering 1877 Metropolitan Open Spaces Act, which gave the body then known as the London Metropolitan Board of Works powers to acquire certain categories of land for leisure use.

In 1878 with a small group of friends and supporters Octavia Hill established the Kyrle Society. The Society was named after the philanthropist John Kyrle, the real-life model for poet Alexander Pope's "Man of Ross" in his Third Moral Essay. The Society became a focal point for Octavia's campaigning work for free public access to many of the normally closed leafy squares and gardens in central London, and the Society worked closely with the Commons Preservation Society and Bob Hunter to save Burnham Beeches, a magnificent woodland close to London. Octavia was also instrumental in the safeguarding of Hampstead Heath, perhaps London's most iconic open space, which was brought into full public ownership in 1889.

The Kyrle Society was able, through Octavia's considerable networking skills, to attract wealthy and aristocratic patrons. This was a strategy which paid rich dividends. Support came from such influential figures as John Ruskin and William Morris, and the Society's campaigning work extended to include safeguarding many historic buildings.

By the 1890s there were countless new opportunities and challenges to protect nationally important properties by acquisition by individual local trusts – including such iconic properties as the former homes of Shakespeare, Milton and Wordsworth.

But with several important country estates at that time up for sale in the heart of the Lake District, Bob Hunter, representing the Commons Preservation Society, was quick to realise that what was needed was an organisation larger and with more resources and influence than the two Societies, to act in what was clearly the national interest to save such places for future generations. On 16 November 1893 Hunter, Hill and Rawnsley called a meeting in the office of the Commons Society to discuss the establishment of what was provisionally called a "National Trust for Historic Sites and Natural Scenery".

Decisions were duly taken to establish a not-for-profit-making Joint Stock Company with a view to acquiring property, including land and properties in the national interest. Hunter and Hill drew up a list of influential people from among the liberal Establishment – the Great and the Good – to serve on the first National Trust Council, with Bob Hunter its first Chairman, Hardwicke Rawnsley its first Honorary Secretary and the Duke of Westminster its first President. Within its first few months of its inaugural meeting the Trust had acquired its first property – a four and a half acre rectangle of land on a crag overlooking the Mawddach estuary near Barmouth.

The Trust's prime objective "To Look after Places of Historic Interest or Natural Beauty permanently for the benefit of the nation across England, Wales and Northern Ireland" remains an inspiring driving force. 623,000 acres or 970 square miles (2,520 square kilometres) of land is currently in Trust ownership. This includes the 25% of the Lake District and 12% of the Peak District National Parks which are now in National Trust ownership, giving these important areas of now fully accessible land national protection far beyond that which they might receive even from being within a National Park. The Trust also safeguards no less than a fifth of the coastline of England and Wales.

But with the rapid expansion of urbanisation and increases in road transport after World War I, came a recognition that the wider countryside of Britain also needed protection through stronger planning laws to resist the constant sporadic, unplanned development which was then occurring. To achieve this in 1926 the Council for the Preservation of Rural England (CPRE) was established largely through the initiative of the leading town planner and architect Patrick Abercrombie (1879-1957), who became its first Secretary. Its mission was to bring together organisations and individuals throughout rural England to protect typical English villages, market towns and the special character and way of life of its countryside, and to gather support for stronger, more effective rural planning laws. It was soon joined by the Association for the Protection of Land in Rural Scotland (APRS) in 1927, and a year later by the Council for the Protection of Rural Wales (CPRW).

CPRE soon became a powerful ally of the National Trust and other outdoor bodies in campaigning for the establishment of National Parks in Britain. The Government responded in 1929 by setting up a Select Committee chaired by the Parliamentary Secretary to the Ministry of Agriculture, Christopher Addison.

With the support of other amenity groups, in November 1929 CPRE convened a National Conference for the Preservation of the Countryside in Manchester that resolved to set up local "National Reserve Committees" in areas

The first motor bus to run in the Yorkshire Dales operated a service between Skipton and Buckden. It is seen outside the Temperance Hotel, Grassington, in the summer of 1908.

A later bus service between Skipton and Leyburn squeezes its way through Bishopdale in the 1930s.

proposed for future National Parks. Such was the enthusiasm for this in the Lake District that at the same weekend a voluntary Lake District National Reserve Committee was formed which included local amenity groups and national and local walking and climbing clubs. The new body, which was eventually to develop, in 1934, into the Friends of the Lake District, not only produced detailed evidence to the Addison Committee for the need for a National Park in the Lake District, but two leading members, Patrick Abercrombie and John Dower, an architect and planner, provided a detailed map of the National Park's potential area and proposed boundaries – which were remarkably similar to those eventually officially adopted.

The Addison Committee duly reported in 1931 and proposed that there should be National Parks Commissions established in England and Wales with a budget of at least £100,000 per annum for five years leading to the setting up of joint regional planning executives. Their role would be "to safeguard areas of exceptional national interest against a) disorderly development and b) spoliation, ii) to improve the means of access for pedestrians to natural beauty and iii) to improve measures for the protection of flora and fauna".

The political and economic situation in Britain in the early 1930s delayed any further action at Government level to develop National Parks. But in 1934 the amenity bodies, by now impatient, took action by using what was the annual meeting of the Ramblers' Federation in Fitz Park, Keswick, as a public rally to further the National Park agenda. During the meeting it was agreed to set up a new body, the Friends of the Lake District, to campaign for the setting up of National Parks in Britain, but in the Lake District as a priority. Speakers at this rally included Patrick Abercrombie, Charles Trevelyan, (Fabian socialist and former Labour MP, brother of G.M.Trevelyan), T.A. Leonard and H.H. "Hal" Symonds, all of whom were or were to become leading national players in the access and National Parks movement.

At the CPRE annual conference in 1935 a motion was passed to establish a "Standing Committee on National Parks". Membership of the new organisation was to come not from individuals but from representatives of leading national amenity groups, including CPRE itself, the National Trust, the newly established Ramblers' Association, the Cyclists Touring Club and Youth Hostels Association. Its first Chairman was Norman Birkett, the famous criminal barrister and a leading light in the Friends of the Lake District, with John Dower its first drafting Secretary. The Standing Committee had its first meeting on 26 May 1936 and was hugely influential in the long process leading to the establishment of National Parks in Britain. In later years it became the Council and more recently the Campaign for National Parks (CNP). CNP remains the leading watchdog for National Parks in the UK, and, over the decades since its foundation, has done more than any other organisation to create and strengthen successive National Park legislation, and to work with politicians of all persuasions to ensure National Parks are properly funded so that they are truly able to realise their objectives.

The National Trust, CPRE, CPRW and CNP are superb examples of how a group of enlightened, highly motivated upper-middle class people from professional backgrounds have successfully campaigned for countryside protection, better planning laws and for the conservation and improved access to historic buildings and open spaces. But there is a different, if complementary, tradition of access campaigning, with its roots in the ordinary, urban lower middle class and working class communities, especially of northern England.

By late Victorian and early Edwardian times, rambling clubs and societies attracting and involving working men and women were springing up in London and many large cities. Manchester YMCA Rambling Club was established in 1880, the Midland Institute of Ramblers in 1894, Liverpool YMCA Rambling Club and Liverpool Hobnails soon afterwards. In 1905 sixteen Clubs in London formed themselves into the London-based Federation of Rambling Clubs with an aim of preserving ramblers' rights and negotiating cheap walkers' excursion tickets on the railways.

By the 1930s the 'big four' railway companies were carrying thousands of ramblers into the countryside. They published comprehensive guidebooks, as shown in this selection.

Especially noteworthy is *Southern Rambles for Londoners* by S P B Mais. This breezy, liberated composition with the girl featured alone, twirling her stick, with her lightweight coat over the shoulder, reflected the sense of the nonchalant freedom of the open countryside that the Southern Railway and their successors presented to Londoners. (A. Bennett Collection and R. Bryant Collection – this page, bottom left, and opposite, bottom right)

RAMBLES IN SOUTH DEVON
By HUGH E. PAGE
RAMBLES IN THE WYE VALLEY
Hugh E. Page
1/-
RAMBLES IN the WYE VALLEY
by Hugh E. Page... 6D
RAMBLES IN SOUTH DEVON
Hugh E. Page
1/-
RAMBLES AROUND the CAMBRIAN COAST
by Hugh E. Page. 6D
RAMBLES IN THE CHILTERN COUNTRY
BY HUGH E. PAGE

The links between early socialists, evangelical Christians and walking was a strong one, a form of "muscular Christianity" as popularised by Leslie Stephen with a love of plain living and high thinking which permeates the rambling fraternity to the present day.

T. Arthur Leonard was a Congregational Minister in the mill town of Colne, Lancashire, who had a rambling club branch within his church social club. He felt that a week's walking in the Lake District could offer much more to the youngsters of his parish than a similar week in the more sedentary attractions of Blackpool. In 1891 he took a group of young men from Colne for a week's walking holiday in the Lake District. He soon began organising similar holidays to wider groups of young people. The enterprise began life under the name of the Co-operative Holidays Association, later known as Countrywide Holidays Association or CHA. Initially the CHA rented accommodation, in 1896 taking out a five-year lease on its first property, Abbey House in Whitby, but later was able to purchase property. By 1911 the CHA had 14,000 members, and by 1931 was operating from a total of 18 centres. The CHA was one of the world's first organisations to provide organised walking holidays – which continued until the 1990s, in both UK and abroad, before being absorbed first into the Shearings organisation and finally into Ramblers' Holidays.

However in 1913 Arthur Leonard decided that the organisation he had created had become too large and had lost its ideals, in that the poorer young people he originally sought to attract could no longer afford the more comfortable accommodation now available. He believed there should be a greater emphasis on affordable and simpler "youth camps" and cheaper mountain-hut style accommodation which youngsters from the cities could afford. He therefore resigned and immediately set about, with a group of friends, establishing the Holiday Fellowship – the HF. The CHA and HF continued to work together amicably, with the CHA offering their centre at Newlands in the Lake District for use by the HF at generous terms.

The HF Holidays is now a highly successful worldwide outdoor holiday organisation, with high quality centres which perhaps do not quite share Arthur Leonard's belief in the simple life, but provide excellent holidays and companionship for ramblers of all ages. The CHA's and HF's local branches survive as independent social and walking clubs throughout the UK, taking an active part in the work of the Ramblers' Association, as affiliated clubs, on a local level.

Following the London example, Federations of Rambling Clubs were formed during the 1920s in the Manchester area, in Liverpool, Sheffield and in the early 1930s in Bolton, Leicestershire, Lincolnshire, the Midlands, Nottinghamshire and the West Riding. In 1931 it was agreed to establish the National Council of Ramblers' Federations. In 1935 the National Council became more simply and memorably the Ramblers' Association.

But if walking clubs were flourishing like never before, encouraged by the popularity of the Scouting movement, established by Robert Baden-Powell in 1908, so was the new phenomenon of "hiking" – a word which gained new currency from its use in the United States. It became a popular term among a newly energised working class who, in the years after World War I, poured out from the cities on the excursion trains and regular Sunday train services into the nearby countryside.

It was estimated that on a fine Sunday up to 15,000 people could pile on trains in Manchester and a similar number from Sheffield on trains along what is now known as the Hope Valley Line between Manchester and Sheffield, through the heart of the Peak District. Bolton Abbey Station in the Yorkshire Dales had an estimated 8,000 walkers alighting on a typical fine Sunday or Bank Holiday. Even as late as the 1950s, the village of Grassington was reportedly "eaten out" by walkers and other visitors who had arrived in huge numbers by special excursion trains on Bank Holidays along the little branch railway from Skipton, travelling from Manchester, Leeds and Bradford, and were seen in their hundreds picnicking by the river.

A special train brings ramblers to Kirbymoorside station in May 1964 three months before closure of this line in Ryedale. Two conducted rambles – both of sixteen miles and described as 'strenuous' – had been organised and had to be completed in six hours. (T E Walker)

As that great champion of public access and the rambling cause Professor Cyril Joad of BBC Radio Brains Trust fame, wrote in 1933:

Those of us who live in the south have little conception of the hold which the "rambling" movement has had on the young people of the north. The Central Station in Manchester early on a Sunday morning is an unforgettable sight; with its crowds of ramblers, complete with rucksacks, shorts, and hob-nailed boots, waiting for the early trains to Edale, Chinley, Hope and the Derbyshire moors, it might lead one to suppose that the whole of Manchester was in exodus. And it is, indeed, true that this generation has replaced beer by "hiking" as the shortest cut out of Manchester.

Another major part of the outdoor movement which encouraged many more young working class people to get out and enjoy the countryside like never before was the Youth Hostels Association. Youth Hostelling was the inspiration of a young German schoolteacher Robert Shirrman, who in 1909 saw a need to encourage young people to get out of the huge new industrial cities of Germany, such as those of the mighty Ruhr region, into the hills and mountains of the Black Forest, Thüringen and the Harz by providing a network of hostels offering cheap, clean accommodation – the Jugendherbergen.

It took another 20 years for the concept to take root in Britain, with Liverpool and Merseyside taking the lead, and the formation in 1930 of the British Youth Hostels Association, with G.M. Trevelyan as its first President. This soon became the Youth Hostels Association (England and Wales) with Scotland and Northern Ireland electing to have their own organisations. The first Youth Hostel in Britain was at Pennant Hall near Llanrwst in 1930, which sadly had soon to close because of water contamination, but by 1931 there were already 75 hostels open throughout England and Wales.

Youth Hostels, once much more numerous than today, played a significant role in the growth of the outdoor movement. This group of ramblers, very much dressed in a style now a victim of fashion, takes advice from the warden outside Lastingham Youth Hostel. (Geoffrey N Wright)

It cost just 5/- a year (25p) to become a Senior Member (over 25) but a Junior (under 25) was just 2/6d (12½). The cost of a night in a YHA hostel (bring your own sheet or sleeping bag though blankets and pillows were provided) was just 1/- (5p) for Seniors and 6d (2½p) for a Junior. Costs were kept to a minimum by hostellers doing chores to clean and maintain the hostels.

Little wonder that by the outbreak of World War II the YHA had 83,000 members, and 600,000 annual bed night stays at hostels were being recorded. Membership and activity soared during the 1950s, passing the 200,000 membership mark with well over a million overnight stays. The YHA soon became a major campaigning body for better access for cyclists and walkers in the countryside, a role that continues to this day.

Social change, emancipation and the experience of a devastating World War made this new generation far less nervous of authority or subservient to land owners or farmers than their parents were. Some of the urban "trippers", as the more experienced ramblers labelled them, brought problems with them as they disgorged in large numbers at fine weekends and Bank Holidays from railway stations and later from bus or coach stops. The new arrivals from the towns and cities had little local knowledge of their whereabouts nor did they receive any friendly guidance when they arrived. With little understanding of the life of countryside, and years before the publication of the Country Code, many had no idea of the reasons for the simplest standards of behaviour in the countryside – why it was damaging to trample crops or meadows, to leave gates open or climb fences or walls, leave unsightly or dangerous litter, let their dogs off the leash or even light fires.

Such ignorance and thoughtlessness even if only by a minority of visitors were enough to give constant ammunition to generations of farmers, gamekeepers and their landlords, determined to do everything they could to keep walkers out of their pastures, meadows or away from the grouse moors.

Rather than work to welcome the new arrivals and educate them in rural ways, teaching them to understand and respect the countryside, the reactions of most farmers and landowners, perhaps understandably, were largely hostile and negative. This was especially true of many of the larger landowners, shooting syndicates and their gamekeepers who controlled huge areas of Britain's unenclosed uplands – the mountains of Scotland and Wales, the moorland and fells of Northumberland, the Pennines, North York Moors, Exmoor, Dartmoor and most explosively of all given the size of nearby catchment populations, the Peak District.

The Lake District – by a happy accident with much of its moorland areas Urban Common with full legal right of public access – suffered less problems than the drier, eastern areas of the Peak and Pennines. Here grouse shooting on specially created and protected heather moors by landowners or by wealthy shooting syndicates, covered huge areas close to many of the towns and cities where the majority of people lived and worked. Water Boards, even though they were publicly owned by Corporations from the same cities where the hikers lived and worked, were equally hostile, believing that the presence of walkers on their gathering grounds was a certain source of pollution and contamination of public water supplies. Most of these grouse moors and water catchment grounds were crossed by few, if any, public footpaths or tracks, which made them inaccessible except by trespassing.

As shooting of deer and grouse in the uplands, and pheasants in the lowland woods, had by the 1930s become more popular among the wealthy and therefore more profitable for landowners, so measures to prevent casual access became more ferocious and conflict more serious. Though there was, and is, some risk to wildlife and game resulting from public access, there are a range of simple management and educational measures that can be used to reduce such risks. As National Park Authorities in areas like the Peak District, Exmoor, Dartmoor, North York Moors and Yorkshire Dales have demonstrated so very effectively since the 1960s, much more can be achieved by gaining the public's active co-operation, through education and involvement, for example at times of nesting or periods of high fire risk, than by crude blanket bans and threatening notices. In fact, responsible walkers on the moors are more likely to police the ignorant or less responsible, whereas deserted areas give greater licence for irresponsible behaviour on all sides, including gamekeepers who may be tempted to trap or poison protected birds of prey. Access and conservation are not mutually incompatible.

But by the 1930s antagonism between those who wanted to walk the northern hills, and those who wished to safeguard them exclusively for game conservation, shooting or water catchment, had reached a flash point, with walkers being threatened at gun point, suffering verbal abuse, manhandled off the moors or intimidated with notices threatening legal prosecution.

Legal attempts to secure the right to walk the hills by Parliamentary means went as far back as James Bryce's pioneering Access to Mountains (Scotland) Bill of 1884. With a House of Commons and House of Lords that strongly reflected landowning and farming interests, this and subsequent Bills were defeated, if not in the Commons, then in the Lords. But even mountaineering and rambling organisations were split on the issue, ramblers in the south of England regarding the northern pre-occupation with access to unenclosed moorland as being less relevant to them in the more intensively cultivated south, whilst others were concerned about the dangers of alienating influential farming and landowning interests by appearing too militant.

On Kinder Scout, a bleak area of open moorland, the heartland of what is accurately described as the Dark Peak in Derbyshire, the battle for access to unenclosed uplands entered a whole new phase when a major demonstration took place which was to symbolise the whole "right to roam" debate, pushing it towards class warfare and confrontation. It started in 1932 when the Communist-inspired British Workers' Sports Federation, had a group of their members on an Easter walking trip brutally turned back by a group of gamekeepers on a path near Bleaklow, close to Kinder summit. Angered by the reaction, back at the campsite the frustrated walkers agreed that if there had been enough walkers there that day, the gamekeepers would not have won the day.

So the famous Kinder Trespass came to pass. On 24 April 1932, around 400 ramblers met in Hayfield, a village on the western edge of the Peak District. Among them was a 20 year old unemployed motor mechanic from Cheetham Hill, Manchester, Benny Rothman, who was to

Right: The Kinder Scout Mass Trespassers, 1932. (Peak District National Park)

Below: Benny Rothman, access campaigner, examines a disputed right of way in the West Pennine Moors. (Paul Salveson)

become both a martyr and an icon of the outdoor movement in Britain. Benny was among the leaders of the group as they set out to Bowden Bridge Quarry, and after an impromptu, impassioned speech from Benny continued up the Kinder Road to Nab Brow and William Clough, where at Sandy Heys, on open ground on the side of Kinder, the trespass occurred. A line of twenty to thirty gamekeepers were waiting for them on the edge of the open moor.

What actually happened was subject to much later dispute and misinterpretation. The group headed up the hillside to confront the keepers. There was some scuffling, a keeper was slightly hurt, and the trespassers pressed their way onto the open moor. After meeting up with a group from Sheffield who had walked over Kinder in the other direction to meet them, the trespassers walked back to Hayfield only to find police officers waiting for them. Six people were initially arrested, including one innocent bystander who had merely turned up to witness the incident, and had actually run across the disputed moor to help Edward Beevers, the injured keeper.

At the trial at Derby Assizes, riddled it was alleged with "class prejudice", the five defendants were charged with public order offences, not with trespass, and given gaol sentences of between two and six months.

The severity of the sentences imposed on these young working men and the hardship they suffered in Leicester gaol would ironically lead to the real victory. Even people little concerned for freedom of the fells or access to the moors were appalled by the severity of the sentences received. Whilst the official rambling bodies played down the achievement of what were considered a group of left wing hot-heads, the whole episode gave new input to the wider access movement and the growing campaign for the establishment of British National Parks.

As a result of the huge press publicity, an official (and legal) access rally sponsored by the newly established National Council of Ramblers' Federations a few weeks later in The Winnats Pass, near Castleton, attracted a massive crowd of 10,000. Other mass trespasses took place later that year in the Peak District at Abbey Brook in Upper Derwentdale, and at Stanage Edge on the outskirts of Sheffield, but significantly no arrests were made.

The Winnats Pass Rally became the first of several annual rallies to support the concept of free access to moorlands and mountains. Two years later, in 1934, a key speaker at the third of these rallies was a young man who was a newly appointed editor of the Hiker and Camper magazine, and also the recently appointed open-air correspondent of the Daily Herald, a national newspaper with Labour Party sympathies. His name was Tom Stephenson.

Tom, from Burnley, Lancashire, was one of the truly great countryside campaigners. He was the first major campaigner to be "of the people", born in 1893 into an impoverished working class family, a man who never lost touch with his roots nor his warm, East Lancashire accent. Imprisoned in the First World War as a conscientious objector (which denied him a scholarship in geology at the Royal College, London), Tom was a lifelong pacifist but brilliant if often underrated campaigner for access, walking and National Parks. He used his regular column in the left-wing Daily Herald to widely promote the ramblers' cause, including the concept of a Pennine Way.

It seemed as if the ramblers' cause had been won when in 1938 the MP for Shipley, Arthur Creech Jones, in response to Stephenson's many articles, presented a radical Access to Mountains Bill to the Commons, which Stephenson urged all Herald readers to write to their MP to support. But when the Bill emerged from the various Committee stages it was unrecognisable, in Stephenson's words "not a ramblers' charter but a landowners' protection bill". Worst of all were clauses which made a simple act of trespass – walking on someone's land – a criminal offence.

The Ramblers' Association was totally split on the issue, some senior members urging acceptance of the offensive parts of the Bill to secure the more acceptable measures, others including Stephenson, urging the rejection of all of it. The Bill became law in 1939 but the outbreak of World War II made the Act meaningless.

It also gave Stephenson and his allies chance to achieve the Access to the Mountains Act he felt the country needed, even during the darkest years of World War II. By 1943 he had left his post on the Daily Herald and had become a press officer of the new Ministry of Town and Country Planning but was then free to join the Executive Committee of the Ramblers' Association, eventually becoming its inspiring and long serving Secretary from 1948 to 1969.

How Tom Stephenson used his influence as a young press secretary within the corridors of power both within Whitehall and Westminster is a remarkable story. Tom, a supreme pragmatist, fully understood the political process and was able to influence a group of key people both during the latter stages of the War and in the early post-War years within the Attlee Government. As early as 1942 the Scott Committee's Land Utilisation in Rural Areas Report – which had the leading academic Professor Dudley Stamp as its Vice Chairman – supported the concept of safeguarding key rural areas as National Parks. Significantly, this would not be as American-style "wilderness" Parks, but achieving a compromise with private landowners by controlling development and securing access on foot in various ways.

By 1943 Tom, no longer restrained by his undertaking to the Daily Herald newspaper not to be active in campaigning work, was able to move adroitly between the Ramblers' Association Executive Committee's Access to Mountains sub-committee on which he served and his official work as a "non political" press officer for the Ministry. He won his battle within the Ramblers to support a totally new Act to replace the hated 1939 Access to Mountains Act, then worked with government civil servants and later politicians to get this new Act on the statute book. One of his great friends and allies was fellow northerner John

John Dower.

Dower (1900-47), Secretary of the Standing Committee on National Parks, who was asked to write a report – published in 1945 and now generally known as the Dower Report – about what action should be taken to create National Parks in England and Wales. As Tom was later to record:

The Ministry of Town and Country Planning was a cheerless place permeated by a fear of publicity. John Dower was my only kindred spirit and publicising his famous national parks report in 1945 was one of the most satisfying tasks I ever had. The climate of the time came out clearly at the small monthly planning dinners, followed by a speech and discussion. When Dower spoke, some planners could see no reason for barring motorways from national parks. When I spoke on access to the countryside it was clear that the rights of the rambler were a featherweight against the rights of property. A small Pennine Way exhibition in the entrance hall of the ministry attracted considerable attention and some press comment. This led one assistant secretary to complain that all this publicity about a Pennine Way might lead to a demand for something to be done about it.

But the landslide election of a Labour Government in 1945 paved the way for some of the most profound social changes in Britain's history – in health, education, housing, transport and town and country planning, including the creation of National Parks and related aspects of access to the Countryside.

John Dower's seminal report chimed closely with this mood for social change and a more egalitarian attitude to countryside access:

National Parks should be in a true and full sense national if they are to be worthy of their name and purpose. This does not mean that local interests are to be disregarded. On the contrary, the well-being of those who live and work within them must always be a first consideration. But it does mean that their holiday and recreational uses should be for people – and especially young people – of every class and kind and from every part of the country, indeed of the world....
National Parks are not for any privileged or otherwise restricted section of the population, but for all who come to refresh their minds and spirit and to exercise their bodies in a peaceful setting of natural beauty.

Tom Stephenson was able to gain immediate political support for these ideals among members of the incoming Government, with a firm ally in Lewis Silkin, the new Minister for Town and Country Planning, who encouraged Stephenson to issue a press statement suggesting that some of the finest scenery of Britain could only be enjoyed by trespassers. He also pledged his support for major new legislation, dramatically to revise footpath law, to create new provisions to access to wild places and create both National Parks and long distance footpaths such as the Pennine Way.

Silkin asked Stephenson to join Sir Arthur Hobhouse's committee on National Parks, where he served with John Dower and Francis Ritchie of the Ramblers. This committee which reported in

The Cairngorms, one of the two National Parks finally designated in Scotland. It offers superb opportunities for walkers to explore wild spaces. (Dorian Speakman)

1947 supported all Dower's key recommendations, and those of the Standing Committee, by including the immensely important measure to survey and record all public footpaths in England and Wales to prepare a "Definitive Map" of all known public rights of way.

Then came a disquieting time when it was rumoured that with so much other pressing legislation, there would not be time to get the proposed National Parks and Access to the Countryside Bill on the statute book before the next election due in 1950.

With plenty of covert and open hostility from landowning interests hoping to delay the Act to await an incoming, more landowner-friendly Conservative administration, Stephenson had to act quickly. He not only organised a brilliant letter-writing campaign to MPs from ramblers and other sympathisers, but with the help of a young MP and Fabian Socialist from South Shields, Arthur Blenkinsop, he organised a three day walking trip from Edale along the proposed Pennine Way. MPs who took part included Hugh Dalton, former Chancellor of the Exchequer and at that time Chancellor of the Duchy of Lancaster, and a senior, highly influential Cabinet member (and also President of the RA); Barbara Castle, a rising left-wing firebrand; Fred Willey, later to be Minister of Land and Natural Resources; and Arthur Blenkinsop himself.

This historic walk resulted in Hugh Dalton's determination to secure, within the lifetime of the Government, the necessary legislation. In due course, with highly effective lobbying of sympathetic MPs by three specially deputed Members of the Standing Committee on National Parks – Tom Stephenson, Francis Ritchie and

Tom Stephenson leading a party of MPs along the Peak District section of the proposed Pennine Way, 1948. (Ramblers' Association)

H.H. Symonds – most of the core recommendations of both Dower and Hobhouse were in the Bill which finally became law in December 1949 - the historic and still immensely significant National Parks and Access to the Countryside Act 1949.

Not only did this Act lead to the creation of Britain's still growing family of National Parks, but the establishment of their close and increasingly important cousins, Areas of Outstanding Natural Beauty. This far-reaching, far-seeing Act also established perhaps the world's best-protected network of public footpaths and bridleways, requiring every county in England and Wales to prepare and update a detailed record – the Definitive Map of Rights of Way. There were also powers to create long distance footpaths to access this newly protected countryside – now known as National Trails – and even establish accommodation and ferries to serve them. Nature conservation was also given a huge boost through the establishment of National Nature Reserves. Equally important were the key government agencies to deliver the Act which started life as the National Parks Commission and Nature Conservancy , later the Countryside Commission and English Nature, combined in 2006 into Natural England, with matters in Wales now being dealt with by the Countryside Council for Wales.

The creation of English and Welsh National Parks, Areas of Outstanding Natural Beauty, National Nature Reserves, the Pennine Way and other National Trails, all owe their existence to the 1949 Act. National Parks were not a British invention, despite the germinating idea for " a sort of national property" coming from an English poet. The world's first National Park, Yellowstone, was created in the mountains, canyons and lakes of Wyoming in 1872. It took almost another 80 years before the UK's first National Park was established in 1951 – two years after the 1949 Act in the Peak District. The Lake District, which many thought would have been the nation's first National Park. soon followed, and then Snowdonia. There are now fifteen National Parks in Britain – nine in England, (including the Broads which though not legally a National Park enjoys quasi-National Park Status), three in Wales and, finally, two in Scotland.

It is sobering to reflect that when the 1949 Act was passed, Britain was suffering economically in ways which make the financial problems of the present era laughable. Emerging from an exhausting war against international fascism which left the nation virtually bankrupt, there were serious shortages of housing, food and basic necessities of life beyond the comprehension of the present consumerist generation. Yet it was in the midst of that horrifying war that John Dower, living in Kirkby Malham in the heart of the Yorkshire Dales, wrote his visionary report which laid the foundations for the truly accessible, magnificently protected countryside we all enjoy today. The 1949 Act also encapsulates educational principles deep within its core purposes – to allow people mainly from urban Britain to understand and appreciate a natural and cultural heritage which belongs to them every bit as much as it does to privileged elites.

Sadly, John Dower died in 1947 and did not live to see his visionary report turned to reality. Tom Stephenson however continued to have, as the first full-time paid Secretary of the Ramblers, a strong influence on the implementation of the 1949 Act with its many triumphs, but its inevitable disappointments as rural local authorities in particular sought to weaken or ignore its measures over such issues as footpath protection, access to open country and even independent National Parks.

Inevitably there were compromises and serious weaknesses in the Act. There were local authorities, especially many County Councils who saw their bureaucratic empires threatened by the establishment of National Parks within their territories, and public Water Boards who fiercely resisted all access to their gathering grounds. The National Park Commission was itself under-funded and lacking in powers – a situation only remedied in 1968 when it became the Countryside Commission. A loophole in the legislation also allowed toothless "Joint Advisory Committees" or single committees to be set up to manage National Parks instead of the powerful, independent Boards originally intended. This was an anomaly only put right, after constant lobbying by CNP, CPRE, the RA and others, by the 1995 Environment Act. But a proposal in the Hobhouse Report for an income of one million pounds per annum from the national Land Fund for National Parks was quietly dropped by Government and National Parks remained grossly underfunded for a generation. Outside the Peak District and one relatively small area of the Yorkshire Dales, the Access measures of the 1949 Act, as we shall see in the next chapter, were largely ignored.

But there were victories. One former National Park Officer, Derek Statham, has written a fascinating account – *An Eye to Perceive* (the title quoting Wordsworth) – of how his own North York Moors National Park Authority gradually evolved over 20 years from being in 1974 a mere Committee of a County Council, to in 1995 achieving a degree of independence. This independence, supported by committed, specialist staff, allowed his Authority to work with landowners and farmers in new and innovative ways to protect the moorland and to achieve conservation, access and land management objectives that have now become standard practice in protected landscapes throughout Britain and even overseas.

Much of this progress was only possible because over the last 60 years since the passing of the 1949 Act, the amenity organisations led by the Campaign for National Parks have continued to pressurise Governments of the two major political parties to constantly re-legislate to improve and adapt National Parks and countryside legislation to meet the needs of a changing world, and also to ensure adequate funds were available to deliver what that legislation promised. Perhaps the most significant of all was the Countryside and Rights of Way Act 2000 – the so-called CROW Act – which finally achieved the intended universal access to moorland and mountains in England and Wales.

But in essence the effect of this new legislation has been to strengthen and clarify the "unfinished business" of the 1949 Act. Much of the Act remains as relevant and as important to the people of Britain as it was in the 1940s. Even with its weaknesses, it was and has proved to be, a true "Ramblers' Charter", fulfilling the vision and promises made during all those years of protest on Berkhamsted Common, Latrigg Fell, Kinder Scout, Ilkley Moor or Winnats Pass.

So even though it took more than half a century to achieve, the spirit of the 1949 Act has eventually triumphed, a living tribute to the great countryside campaigners, poets and ramblers of the last two centuries, to whom Britain's present and future generations of walkers owe an immense and continuing debt of gratitude.

Walkers and cyclists enjoy The Ridgeway, a prehistoric highway between Ivinghoe Beacon, Buckinghamshire and Avebury, Wiltshire that still enjoys ancient rights for walkers, cyclists and vehicle users. (Natural England: Ann Seth)

4. PATHS, MAPS AND THE FREEDOM TO ROAM

To walk along a footpath through a cornfield on a Sunday evening in summer, with the sound of bells ringing the people to church, is an experience as unforgettable as it is unique. No other country can match it – Cyril Joad

If you stand on a hillside in almost any area of rural Britain, and look across at the landscape stretched out before you, the oldest single man-made feature of that landscape may not be the walls, hedges, barns, farmhouses or even castles, nor even the less decipherable ridges or mounds, relics of old field systems, stone quarries or even habitations left by our long vanished forefathers.

A path or track which slants its way up the hillside, crosses the ridge, its route incised into the landscape by generations of feet or hooves, may pre-date all of these things. And very likely it is still in use, a footpath or bridleway, attracting walkers, horse riders and even cyclists.

Footpaths and bridlepaths are as old and sometimes older than England, Scotland or Wales. Some go back to the dawn of our civilisation to the time of early hunter-gatherers who followed the higher land between the impenetrable forest and swamp that covered the valleys of much of post-Ice Age Britain, or early farmers who established the first prehistoric trade routes, still decipherable as ridgeways and high moorland tracks. A very substantial percentage of surviving country paths go back to Anglo-Saxon, Viking or later medieval times of the first settlement of modern villages, paths beaten out by people walking between outlying homesteads and farms to the larger "tuns"

A footpath squeezes between Enclosure walls, Upper Wharfedale.

A narrow stile allows the Coast to Coast Path to squeeze through a drystone Enclosure wall in Swaledale.

A 17th century guide post, which still marks the medieval "Badgergate" or Pedlars' Path that crosses the Nidderdale moors en route between Halifax and Knaresborough.

or villages, fording rivers or leading to the nearest church or burial ground, which are still sometimes known as "parishioners' way". The folk-myth of a path being created over the line taken by coffins being carried to a graveyard has a germ of truth in that footways to consecrated ground, hollowed and hallowed by usage, often remain as public paths to this very day.

Many later paths date from the time of Enclosure, when perhaps myriads of paths and trackways over open fields and common land were channelled into defined paths, marked by stiles and gates built into the Enclosure walls or hedges and legally defined by the particular Enclosure Award. One reason why farmers and landowners still have the responsibility to maintain stiles and gates is that a wall or hedge built to enclose a field is technically an obstruction and the maintaining of a stile or gate in good condition to allow free passage over that obstruction is therefore a legal duty.

Other old green ways had evolved from paths to broader bridleways or drove ways, some of them used by packhorses or driven cattle, sheep or even geese, capable of taking steeper more direct routes than wheeled vehicles, many of them falling out of usage when new, level turnpike roads were built mainly in the 18th and early 19th centuries for faster carriages. Others evolved to become waggon and carriage ways, or the winding networks of country lanes, now tarmacadamed and widened for use by modern motor traffic. But many of the older, unimproved routes have retained their bridleway status, and are increasingly important for non-motorised traffic, for walkers, cyclists and horse riders.

Highway law, and footpath law in particular, is a fascinating, complex study, its origins going back as it does to the roots of English civilisation, to Anglo-Saxon common law defined from the time of Alfred the Great. Despite recent changes in legislation (the Countryside and Rights of Way Act 2000), the ancient concept of "once a highway always a highway" still has some legal force. If it can be proved, in a court of law, that a path or road has enjoyed uninterrupted and unchallenged use for a period of twenty years – not just from the present but at any such period of time since 1 January 1949 – neither merely by permission, nor against the clearly expressed wish of the landowner, then this is powerful evidence in a court of law that a right of way still exists over that land. However, the CROW Act 2000 has determined that ancient, pre 1949 rights which have not been registered as rights of way by January 1st 2026 will be extinguished unless recorded on Definitive Maps as footpaths, bridleways or byways. Many people have questioned the wisdom of changing what has, until now, been a fundamental part of our democratic rights.

But footpaths remain a part of our very thought process. The very word "way" as a means of achieving a goal, is built into our language as a concept. A right of way is just that – a means of achieving a journey, reaching a destination.

Even land ownership, as the environmental writer Marion Shoard has argued, is a concept which only goes back to the Norman Conquest. The post-Norman belief of absolute control over a piece of territory is in fact a property right subject to certain rights which may be held by other individuals (such as in individual's way-leave across one owner's land to another owner's or lessee's property or mineral rights) or by the state or indeed by the public at large. A right of way across someone's land is therefore not in any way a concession but a fundamental part of our democratic rights as citizens, though naturally such rights can and should only be exercised with due responsibility.

A right of way is therefore exclusively a right of passage along a defined route. Width of a path is not defined in law as it may vary according to usage and to physical conditions. A yard – 3 feet – is often assumed as reasonable for a footpath, 5 feet for a bridleway, though this is often defined by local authorities in a metric age as one metre for footpath and two metres for a bridleway. Right of way status does not give the walker a right to stray off the route, though in practice if you stop to take a photograph or even stop for a picnic, this can be interpreted as being a "reasonably incidental" purpose to your right of passage, and is therefore allowed.

The concept of a "highway" goes back to the time when early constructed roads, from Roman times onwards, were raised slightly above the surrounding land for draining purposes, and usually paved or "metalled". But the term has come to include all public rights of way, even quite narrow footpaths and unsurfaced tracks, as well as bridleways and carriageways – i.e. highways where there is a right to take a wheeled vehicle.

Rights of way follow a careful hierarchy, starting with the most simple, the humble footpath which gives right of passage on foot only, and dogs if under control.

The second tier is that of the bridleway, which includes foot traffic, but also right of passage on horseback and by cycle.

These two categories are the most significant and important types of rights of way for walkers.

So far, so good. But then come the higher categories. The most important of these is the Byway, as it name implies, the least busy type of minor public road. They may or may not be surfaced or metalled, and many were in fact classified in the past as "Roads Used as Public Paths" or RUPPs. Byways differ from bridleways in that wheeled vehicles (not just pedal cycles) have a right to use them, and can also be described as a Carriageway. Recent legislation makes the distinction between Byways Open to All Traffic (BOATS), which as their name implies can be used by all motorised vehicles – cars, 4x4s, motorbikes, as well as horse riders, cyclists and walkers, and a Restricted Byway.

The new concept of a Restricted Byway indicates that this particular type of Byway can only legally carry non-motorised traffic, that is walkers, cyclists, horse riders, and horse drawn vehicles, which in many cases was the actual "vehicular" use of such old roads as sanctified by tradition.

So how does a walker or for that matter a farmer or landowner know where a right of way runs? A footpath is not necessarily something that can be seen on the ground – it takes a lot of regular, constant pedestrian traffic to wear even a narrow physical path through covering vegetation. Most footpaths, especially those that are only lightly used, are difficult to see on the ground, if there are no signposts or stiles.

One of the towering achievements of the 1949 Access to the Countryside Act was to require all local authorities to prepare what was named as the Definitive Map of Rights of Way in their area.

It was a long, slow process which took over two decades to complete. Some commentators have argued, with justification, that the system was biased against urban walkers by focusing on parishes and parish meetings for evidence of the existence of public rights of way, even though hundreds of walkers living in a nearby town or even the next village may have walked the routes in question into their neighbouring countryside all their lives.

Parish Councils were asked by their local authority to mark up on what became known as a Draft Map of footpaths and bridleways in their parish. Some parishes were very conscientious – especially if there was a keen local walker on the Council – and dutifully used their local knowledge and those of people in their parish to record all known public paths. Others, however, especially where there was only a Parish Meeting, usually chaired by the local major landowner him or herself, the job of recording the paths was less well done. Many village people took the erroneous view that as they were "locals" they could walk the paths in their village without asking permission from the local farmer or estate owner, so there was no good reason to put such paths on the map only to encourage strangers to walk there.

I recall as a young volunteer trying to gather evidence for the West Riding Area of the Ramblers' Association from local people in a large village on the edge of the Yorkshire Dales, to ensure otherwise forgotten footpaths would be put on the West Riding County Council Draft Footpath Map for that village. Many local villagers were unwilling to give evidence which might jeopardise their relationship with local estate owners who might also own the house they lived in. Country people also tend to be suspicious of outsiders and not be prepared to upset their neighbours by making a very public, signed statement that they have used a particular village path for over 20 years. Nevertheless I found two people in the village who were less intimidated by the local squire. One was the schoolteacher, whose job and home didn't depend on grace and favour, the other a retired railway worker. The evidence they were able to offer subsequently enabled some key footpaths to be recorded on the Draft Map.

The Draft Map was subject to a quasi-judicial process of public hearings with an Inspector, where landowners and occupiers could object to the inclusion of a path on the Map, often supported by estate workers very willing to swear that paths they had used all their lives were not in fact public, but only used with permission from the great house. However, local authorities and the public could and did on many occasions provide evidence to the contrary. Equally important from the walkers' viewpoint, ramblers could ask for paths omitted from the Draft Map to be included, but they invariably had to provide good evidence to support their case. This was usually in the form of at least six or more signed statements from older people (not just those living in the parish) who could claim to have used the path for over twenty years, in full belief that it was a public right of way. Alternatively they could produce written evidence either in an Enclosure Award document or other clear, authoritative evidence that a path or old road had existed at some time in the past, the ancient principle of "once a highway always a highway" until it was legally closed, being still a fundamental part of modern highway law.

An example of how this process worked in practice was well illustrated when in 1957 a number of rights of way were claimed by the Ramblers' Association through the 2,000 acres of Haveragh Park, an area of farmland and reservoirs in North Yorkshire. These were opposed by the local Water Board in whose catchment area and over whose land the footpaths went. However, the then West Riding RA's Assistant Footpath Secretary, Corrie Gaunt, was able to produce evidence to the County Council, much of it collected at a public meeting he had arranged with local people. Corrie quoted evidence going back to the 17th century, citing a court case when one William Simpson was accused of an offence because he "did stoppe a common foote way in Long Lees and Upper Close" in the Park, proving beyond doubt that in 1667 at least a public footpath way did indeed exist.

One elderly man recalled his grandparents keeping the local Sun Inn at Norwood at the edge of the Park, and on fine Sundays in his childhood a large number of people walking there along the disputed path from Harrogate, for a one shilling dinner of carved roast meat and Yorkshire pudding. But the cat was really let out of the bag when a farmer, when asked by the Harrogate Water Engineer to state that he had turned ramblers back on the disputed paths, wrote:

I must write the truth about this right of way through Haveragh Park. I lived at Long Liberty Farm for nine years, and I can truthfully say we never turned any ramblers back as long as they kept to the Roman Road and did not go looking for mushrooms or rabbitting.

This overwhelming evidence, much of it gathered at a well supported public meeting with local people, was duly accepted by the County Council. The paths are now busy with ramblers at any time of the week or year, many walking to what is still a popular ramblers' inn.

When this process of recording and evidence gathering was complete, the Provisional Map was published by the County Council and made available to the public. This gave landowners, occupiers or lessees of land a further, final chance to object to the inclusion of any path over their land at a Crown Court hearing (which also included the chance to prove the path was wrongly shown on the map). Local Authorities either had to concede the objection (which often happened) or to defend the case, bringing in members of the public as witnesses. Apart from the right of appeal to the High Court on malpractice concerning the

actual legal process, the results of the Court's deliberations were final, legal proof of the existence or otherwise of a right of way at the time the Draft Map was being prepared.

The document to emerge, after this long and arduous process, was the Definitive Map of Rights of Way for each and every county in England and Wales. Scotland and Northern Ireland were, sadly, not included in this process, having their own administrations dealing with highways and access matters. It was a magnificent achievement, perhaps the most important single document for walkers in any area because it truly gives the rambler almost complete confidence in that he or she knows exactly where they can legally walk. The absence of a path from the Definitive Map is no evidence that it is not a right of way, simply that it has not been proven to be such at the relevant date. The existence of a right of way on the Definitive Map is however full and final, almost unchallengeable evidence, that at the "relevant date" a right of way existed. It could of course have been diverted, closed or a new path opened subsequent to that date but these changes have to be incorporated onto the Definitive Map at the first opportunity, and are then published by the Ordnance Survey in future editions of their Landranger or Explorer Maps.

Celebration walk through Haveragh Park in 1969, when disputed paths were added to the West Riding County Council Definitive Footpath Map. Harrogate Ramblers' Association members are accompanying West Riding RA Joint Footpath Secretary Corrie Gaunt (second left in checked shirt). (Yorkshire Post Newspapers)

Despite the length and complexity of the process, which took in some cases over twenty years to complete, each county of England and Wales finally produced their Definitive Maps. As well as the map (usually but not invariably at a pre-metric six inch to one mile scale – approximately 1:10,000), there is also a "Statement" which is a brief description of each and every path, describing its length and characteristics and giving each path a number within each parish so it can be identified quickly and easily.

In later years the Ramblers' Association were able to point out statistical differences between parishes with larger populations or with sufficient recent incomers less worried about offending their farming or landowning neighbours by recording everything they believed to be a right of way, and those deep rural, more lightly populated parishes where there are large blank areas on the map. They could also show that some more rural counties of England had overall far less paths per square kilometre, compared with those with larger townships among their voters and elected members, and a greater commitment to accessing the countryside.

Technically a landowner can have a path removed from the Definitive Map only if he can prove that it was originally shown in error but this requires new evidence to be produced which it can be demonstrated was not available at the time of the original Definitive Map process.

On the other hand, the Wildlife and Countryside Act 1981 allows local authorities to make what are known as Modification Orders, not only to bring their Definitive Map up to date by incorporating any changes since the original map was prepared in the 1950s – that is closures, diversions or creations of paths – but where there is good evidence that a right of way exists that had not been previously shown, though, as a result of the CROW Act 2000 (Section 53) any ancient, pre-1949 rights of way not recorded by 2026 are immediately extinguished. However, any new rights of way, which may have been created as a result of at least twenty years of uninterrupted use since the original Definitive Map was prepared, can be included.

The powers can also be used to rectify map errors, for example where a path has clearly been shown to run alongside the wrong side of a fence or through the wrong field. The changes can all be incorporated into a single Modification Order. This has to be duly advertised in the local press and on site, and if opposed then the objections to those paths have to be submitted to the Secretary of State who may then hold a local hearing or inquiry to consider the evidence.

Landowners can, and occasionally do, agree to dedicate a footpath or a bridleway through a Footpath or Bridleway Dedication Agreement. This also means that the local authority then has the duty to maintain that route. Local authorities can also create footpaths by Agreement or by using compulsory powers by means of an Order. Sadly, Orders are a mechanism extremely rarely used, even when there is an obdurate landowner or tenant and an overwhelming public need, for example on the grounds of safety where walkers have to risk their lives on what are now extremely busy, fast roads.

The 1949 Act allowed some former County Boroughs – cities and larger towns – to plead exemption from the requirements of the Act to prepare a Definitive Map on the grounds of being largely built up areas, but as we shall see in a later chapter, this was a serious mistake and misconception. Most old pre-1974 County Boroughs are now parts of larger Unitary Authorities which have relented and have duly recorded their full rights of way network in both their former County Council and County Borough areas. As we shall suggest, urban paths are perhaps every bit as important as rural paths, even if they may be used in a slightly different way.

Despite its weakness and shortcomings, the preparation and publication of Definitive Maps of Rights of Way for England and Wales was an astonishing achievement. These are documents that safeguard the democratic right of millions of ordinary people, who do not own land or country estates, to enjoy and experience the countryside over which the paths run. It is a law that defends the right of the weak to share our countryside heritage and protects this right against the rich and powerful who might choose to deny this right. Even multi-billionaires and pop stars, when acquiring their huge country estates and luxury mansions, have not been able to ride roughshod over their legal obligations to allow the right of passage on foot or hoof conferred by the Definitive Map, though it often takes months, even years, to persuade local authorities to take legal action to defend that right.

The Definitive Map is subject, inevitably, to constant, albeit minor changes. It was fortuitous that preparation of the Map occurred at a time when motorisation of the countryside had yet fully

Keeping rights of way open. Footpath checkers cross a potato field next to the A1 at Aberford in June 1974. At the head is Jack Madden followed by Eric Barker – both members of Ramblers' Association footpath groups. (Yorkshire Post Newspapers)

to take place, and there were still plenty of people living deep in rural England and Wales who knew where the footpaths ran and were able and prepared to give evidence and record their experiences. However, from the 1960s onwards rapid expansion of car ownership in rural Britain meant that many once busy local footpaths, though recorded on the official maps, were soon relatively little used and forgotten.

Once the publication of the first maps of rights of way in the 1970s began to appear on the new 1:50,000 Ordnance Survey Maps, and later 1:25,000 maps, walkers could see quickly and easily where the paths were located.

However, in some cases they had become neglected, overgrown and blocked, deliberately or accidentally, by landowners and farmers. Many had been ploughed out, despite requirements for ploughed paths to be restored. In some parts of the country, most notably in East Anglia where hedgerows were removed to create huge "prairie farms" (ironically going back to the older pre-Enclosure landscapes), huge new deep ploughed areas hundreds of metres wide made footpaths unwalkable, or subject to long diversions.

Even if the paths were retained, in such areas they ran through empty, featureless landscapes unattractive to walkers – though if at least some old tracks and lanes have survived it is better for cyclists.

Many walkers also complained that they had to use "commando tactics" to walk some paths. Statistics were produced by the Ramblers' Association to show that in some rural areas, the majority of paths could not be walked without meeting at least one major problem and sometimes

Members of the Campaign for National Parks examine damage done by 4x4 vehicles to Mastiles Lane, the ancient green road between Malham Moor and Kilnsey in the Yorkshire Dales.

David Rubinstein, then Secretary of the East Riding Area of the Ramblers' Association, confronts barbed wire blocking a right of way in the Yorkshire Wolds. In the 1970s blocked paths were a far more frequent hazard than four decades later, though problems can still occur.

several serious obstructions even on a short walk. In some cases many paths were totally obstructed and completely impassable. In many rural counties of England and Wales outside National Parks and Wales such problems remain.

Local authorities, when approached, pleaded lack of resources to undertake the backlog of maintenance. The National Farmers' Union, Country Landowners Association and even some local planning authorities led a campaign for the "rationalisation" of the footpath network, claiming that as many footpaths were no longer needed for their original use by people travelling to work or for social purposes, paths should be simplified, duplication removed and an emphasis placed on a much smaller network of well maintained, strategic "recreation" paths. In some cases , for example in West Sussex and Nottinghamshire during the 1970s, major rationalisation schemes were tried out but the schemes were only partially successful, being both time consuming and ultimately expensive, having been met with strong local resistance and much negative publicity.

The Ramblers' Association led this strong counter-attack, claiming, with some justification, that not only is the right of way network a historic part of our cultural landscape, but future needs could emerge which would justify the retention of paths that at the moment appear to have little or no use. Equally the landowning interests accused the Ramblers of being Luddites and suggested that some changes – usually reductions – to meet changing agricultural and other conditions was essential.

Such changes produce the kind of skeletal network experienced in most other European countries such as France, the Netherlands, and even Scotland and Northern Ireland (which do not have an equivalent of the English and Welsh Definitive Map). Even walker-friendly Germany and Scandinavia have relatively few local paths, mainly well waymarked "recreation" trails mostly in popular visitor areas. However, both Germany and Sweden and to some extent Scotland enjoy much more liberal access laws or the "Betretungsrecht" allowing far greater access over mountains , forests and even along farm tracks and through cultivated areas.

In fact, the law in England and Wales allows local piecemeal agreements to be reached between landowners and users which can, without cumbersome rationalisation schemes, produce benefits for both sides. The key is for all sides to ensure that, as well as diversions and closures, creation agreements are used to give new benefits to walkers as well as to farmers and land managers.

It is possible to modify the footpath network in England and Wales perfectly successfully using existing legislation which, with its checks and balances, can ensure a fair deal for land occupiers and rights of way users. Under the Highways Act 1980, local authorities have powers to create, close and divert public rights of way through a democratic process which includes advertising proposals and if there are objections to those proposals, through a public inquiry, the outcome of which is determined by an Inspector appointed by the Secretary of State.

It is a slow process but one which generally works well to protect the public interest, though not always to protect public rights of way from developers. It is relatively easy under Town and Country Planning Acts and other legislation to

Traffic Regulation Order imposed by the Yorkshire Dales National Park Authority at Long Lane, Clapham – now part of the new Pennine Bridleway.

close or divert a public path to permit development to take place, especially major development such as new motorways, power stations or airports. The best schemes can and should bring benefit to both parties, for example taking a footpath out of a busy, muddy farmyard along a drier, perhaps more attractive path around the edge of the farm, benefiting farmer and walker alike. But this often requires a common sense approach and both sides being prepared to give and take to achieve an outcome that benefits both parties.

In addition, landowners and estate managers – including local authorities in areas they own such as Country Parks – can allow people to enjoy a right of passage over their land without conceding a legal right of way. Many landowners including the major Water Utility companies are prepared to do so, and these are known as "permissive" footpaths or bridleways which can be and are shown on published maps. There can also be permissive cycleways which can be granted over land or even over a legal footpath. Permissive routes can have conditions imposed upon them, the most common being prohibiting dogs

The problem with any permissive path is that if a landowner changes his or her mind, or a new owner takes over, that permission can be withdrawn, perhaps at short notice. This can be a problem when such paths are shown on maps, but that is another issue.

Whilst landowners can permit motor vehicles to use their land, this cannot be done over a footpath or bridleway except by the permission of the local authority (usually for a temporary purpose such as a rally). However, it is perfectly possible for a footpath also to run along a farm or household access road or track where there is private vehicular access to a property, but with the access road also being a public right of way for non-vehicular traffic.

Local Highway Authorities, which in England are the County Councils, and in Wales and parts of England the Metropolitan Districts and Unitary Authorities, have considerable duties and powers to "assert and protect" public rights along all public highways, which include footpaths and bridleways. This includes the duty to maintain a right of way – that is to ensure free passage (though repair to stiles and gates are the landowner's responsibility) and ensure surfaces are passable. They can also improve footpaths to a standard appropriate for the regular usage of the area.

Such improvement is not dependent on the landowner's consent, though invariably it is by far the better course of action to secure such consent and co-operation. Local authorities also have the duty to signpost all public paths where they leave metalled highways, except in such cases where a Parish Council suggests such signing is not necessary. Councils and their agents also have the powers to waymark routes, either with the standard former Countryside Agency approved yellow arrow for footpaths or blue for bridleways or more individual themed waymarks for particular walking or riding routes. Again whilst a landowner's consent is not required for this, waymarks are an extremely effective way of reducing accidental trespass and damage, and most landowners and farmers welcome this measure.

Sadly in the past, and indeed in the present, many local authorities, especially some of the larger rural counties of England and Wales, have neglected these duties, continuing to plead lack of resources or financial cutbacks, which is a smokescreen for the fact that access to the countryside is low on their political agenda. Some authorities on the other hand take their duties extremely seriously, and once again there is an urban/rural split, between those authorities with a sizeable urban population and those which are purely rural.

But perhaps the most notable change in the last two decades centres on the initiative for maintaining and even enhancing rights of way networks. It has moved away from County Council Highway Authorities, for whom maintaining and managing rural public paths has always been the lowest priority when starved of cash and manpower, to countryside recreation managers even within the same local authority. Some of these will typically be a team of rangers or countryside wardens, which may well be based at a local authority's Country Park (another form of countryside access provision arising out of the 1968 Countryside Act) and forming part of its Countryside Service, or be involved with a variety of access schemes in and around the countryside on the edge of towns and cities. Countryside Rangers, understanding the importance of rights of way management, together with volunteers, can often bring a fresh impetus and enthusiasm to the management of a local footpath network.

Equally important are the new perspectives and commitment brought to access and footpath protection by those other major countryside protection bodies which eventually emerged from the great 1949 National Parks and Access to the Countryside Act – National Park Authorities, Areas of Outstanding Natural Beauty (AONBs) Joint Advisory Committees and the Countryside Commission – now Natural England and the Countryside Council for Wales. National Parks embody in a powerful way the twin core themes that lie behind the countryside movement – access to open space and assertion of the rights of way network together with conservation of the landscape and wildlife heritage.

In recent years National Parks have moved away from being largely protectionist in attitude to a wider recognition of the importance of their economic base, focusing on what might be best described as "sustainable" or environmentally responsible tourism. This is based on actively encouraging walking, cycling and horse-riding, together with understanding and respecting the natural and historic environment and local culture. Conservation and recreation are correctly perceived as two sides of the same coin. Ultimately one cannot survive without the other as even the "purest" forms of nature-led conservation have, invariably, a human dimension which cannot remain totally the domain of a privileged elite.

In practical terms this has meant that the footpath and bridleway networks of National Parks, far from being Cinderellas, are now near the top of the agenda, with most National Park Authorities which have enjoyed their own independent administrations since the Environment Act of 1995, now having agency arrangements with their local Highway Authorities for the maintenance and indeed improvement of the footpath and bridleway network.

An important new dimension has now been created under the Road Traffic Regulation Act 1984 and the Natural Environment and Rural Communities Act 2006. These enable local authorities (including National Park Authorities) to impose Traffic Regulation Orders (TROs) in certain circumstances on BOATS and other minor roads, to restrict their use by motorised traffic such as motor cycles and 4x4s. This is an important new development for those who do not want to see the ancient green lanes in areas such as the Yorkshire Dales, the Peak District, Brecon Beacons, Exmoor or North York Moors eroded and damaged by motor vehicles and traffic erosion, together with the noise pollution and visual blight such usage causes.

The results of the greater investment in rights of way management in many National Parks such as the Lake District, Yorkshire Dales, North York Moors, Dartmoor and Snowdonia are impressive to see, with high standards of surface maintenance (countering heavy foot erosion on popular routes), well maintained stiles and gates, (often undertaken on behalf of landowners as a part of upland management or Stewardship agreements), and excellent waymarking and interpretation.

Such quality is increasingly being matched by local authority countryside services outside National Parks in various parts of the UK. Standards are also rising within AONBs and along Heritage Coasts. Though they have far less resources and no "recreation" mandate as such, it is increasingly realised that good recreation management is also good landscape and wildlife habitat management, if only because directing visitors along well signed path networks reduces accidental trespass and damage.

The former Countryside Agency offered support and grants to local groups and local authorities through a variety of schemes such as Parish Paths Partnerships and Millennium Greens to encourage

In popular tourist areas the sheer volume of people now using footpaths can cause serious erosion problems. This view of the approach to Gordale Scar in the 1940s shows walkers scrambling over the grass away from any defined path. Ultimately the grass under foot started to break up and something had to be done.

A heavily eroded footpath recently paved with flagstones close to the summit of Mam Tor, Peak District National Park.

The solution to the problem at Gordale was this restored path constructed from stone to meet the huge increase in visitor numbers.

Countryside Rangers have brought huge improvements to the footpath network. Here Simon Bassindale, a Senior Ranger with the North York Moors National Park, patrols his patch near Sutton Bank. (Yorkshire Post Newspapers)

A signpost on Barden Moor Access Area receives running repairs from Wilf Proctor, the first warden for the former West Riding section of the Yorkshire Dales National Park. (David Joy)

the improvement of local footpath networks and for local village green and open space projects. This support continues in a variety of forms through project funding provided by both CCW and Natural England. Similar schemes are available in Scotland through Scottish Natural Heritage.

These schemes have enabled many National Parks and local authorities, especially local Countryside Ranger Services, to create networks of paths which are more easily accessible to the general public, replacing awkward stiles with kissing gates, making surfaces drier and more user friendly, and in appropriate cases making them wheelchair accessible as part of praiseworthy "Access for All" programmes. These developments will be increasingly vital as the UK population ages, with many more elderly people still wanting to access the countryside, though with arthritic limbs no longer able to easily climb high or narrow stiles which would otherwise be major barriers to access.

The improvement and better management of these recreation routes, especially those to and from car parks in popular recreational areas, have both encouraged and been fuelled by far greater access to private transport. This has resulted in a massive increase in leisure walking over the last three decades. If standards have risen so have expectations. No longer are leisure walkers regarded by local authorities as an eccentric minority, though it can be argued that away from the popular recreational areas, and especially in terms of utilitarian walking, they remain marginalised. But equally, walkers are less likely to tolerate poor standards of footpath maintenance and waymarking.

But what about the other fundamental part of the 1949 Act – access to unenclosed mountains and moorlands? Many people considered this to be a fundamental weakness of the Act in that its Access to Open Countryside implementation measures were left in the hands of local authorities. Initially there were some major promising developments, most notably in the Peak District National Park where a whole portfolio of different Access Agreements was developed, covering some 51,000 acres or 80 square miles of open countryside, including that much fought-over icon Kinder Scout.

In the Yorkshire Dales, Barden Moor and Fell – an area of 15,000 acres of superbly managed open grouse moorland within less than an hour's drive of Leeds and Bradford – was, even after the Yorkshire Dales National Park had been established in 1954, subject to constant conflict and controversy. For years this magnificent area of heather moor – the Egdon Heath of the North – where prime ministers and royalty came each autumn to shoot grouse, was only accessible to walkers with a permit. These had to be obtained in advance from the Chatsworth Estate. West Riding Ramblers' Association organised regular pre-and post-war protest demonstrations on nearby Ilkley Moor to change this situation with little effect.

In response to the Ramblers' constant requests for action, the Minister for Housing and Local Government finally asked the West Riding County Council to enter into negotiations for access, but the County Council's view was that a few additional permissive footpaths over the moorland would suffice. The Ramblers disagreed. By 1958, with little sign of progress, the Ramblers convened a national rally on Ilkley Moor, attended by 2,000 walkers from all over the north of England. The eventual result was an Access Agreement for Barden Moor & Fell, though it took another ten years before the entire Agreement was fully operational. This Agreement has proved a model of its kind, over the years building up excellent relations between the National Park Authority, the Chatsworth Estate and the Ramblers. It provided positive experience to inform and underpin the more universal measures of the CROW Act in 2000.

However most local authorities, with in some cases huge areas of open countryside within their boundaries, did not see public access to the moors as a priority. Most, like the old West Riding, quite openly ignored or neglected their duty to prepare maps of open countryside and potential Access land, knowing that Governments of the time generally sympathised more with landowners than walkers, and were not prepared to force them to act. It was therefore a failure of Government, both local and national, not of legislation.

One area where there was major progress, however, was over common land. There had been a major breakthrough in 1925, as a result of intense pressure from the Commons Society, when the Law of Property Act granted the public full legal right of access for air and recreation to all commons lying wholly or partly within urban and metropolitan areas, with the exception of those held by the armed services, for example for training or exercise. By an interesting quirk, urban commons included many parts of the Lake District which happened to lie within old Urban rather than Rural District Council areas. This was true of many popular areas of much loved open common land close to towns and cities throughout England and Wales where people could freely walk their dogs, fly their kites and picnic.

But there was still much uncertainty as to exactly where all our common lands were, especially during the period after World War II when many commons had been ploughed up for food production during that war. In 1955 a Royal Commission on Common Land was set up to look at the future of commons in England and Wales. Again there was highly effective campaigning work by the Ramblers, including an influential report Save our Commons largely written in 1955 by H.H. "Hal" Symonds (1885-1958), someone who was in Tom Stephenson's words "the finest intellect that ever served the RA" and who was by now President of the Ramblers' Association. This pamphlet formed the basis of the RA's submission to the Royal Commission's report which was published in 1958 and finally led to the hugely important Commons Registration Act of 1965. This required all County Councils to provide a complete register of all common land and village greens in their territory, a "Doomsday Book" of all land in England and Wales that was subject to common rights.

Inevitably it was a huge and exhausting process, with many Parish Councils and individuals painstakingly collecting information and evidence

Ilkley Moor – a famous urban common where walkers have enjoyed unrestricted freedom to roam for generations.

A valley in the Yorkshire Wolds, hitherto closed to walkers, now open for public access on foot through the measures of the CROW Act. (Dorian Speakman)

Celebrating the opening of the new CROW Act Public Access areas in the Yorkshire Dales in 2005.

from numerous written archive and other sources. Heroic work was undertaken by the Commons and Open Spaces Society in providing expert knowledge and legal back up as well as their own members helping with the recording and information gathering for even small areas of roadside "waste" and greens. There was also a public inquiry process at which claims could be objected to by landowners with aggrieved objectors having the right to take appeals to the High Court.

But the Registration process did achieve the feat of recording in detail all known commons in England and Wales. Though constant battles continue to prevent the illegal fencing or destruction of such commons, many thousands of acres of fine open countryside have been safeguarded from development or despoliation for the benefit of present and future generations.

Another key recommendation of the Royal Commission was for full legal right of access on foot being granted to all registered commons even though most commons had presumed "de facto" access – if you knew which land was in fact a common. This was not easy information to discover, and it was not easy for walkers out for a day in the countryside – especially in an area they didn't know – to discover whether or not any particular area of common land had any legal rights or even informal tradition of public access.

This was to change with the incoming Labour Government of 1997 with an early manifesto promise for a new Access to the Countryside Bill which was to achieve legal access to all open countryside, including all common land.

Once again this led to a long period of lobbying and counter lobbying at Parliamentary level. The Ramblers provided concrete, scientific evidence that granting public access to grouse moors or upland grazing did not in fact make a significant difference either to nature conservation nor the amount of game available, countering claims by the Moorland Association, the landowners' representative body. It was proved that grouse population levels were largely determined by other factors, including disease and the weather.

After years of intensive negotiation by the Ramblers, the Countryside and Rights of Way (CROW) Act 2000 finally became law.

It is impossible to overestimate the achievement of the two leading national organisations working for access to open countryside, the Ramblers and the Open Spaces Society. This included not only their campaigning and lobbying over several decades, but in the final stages of the Bill which was to become the CROW Act, the immense detailed legal work by paid and voluntary staff of the two organisations, working with Government Ministers, MPs, civil servants in DEFRA and the Countryside Agency to get the Act onto the statute book. It is a story which has yet to be fully told, and inevitably there had to be compromises which have weakened the potential impacts of the legislation, but it was a towering achievement nevertheless.

Action was now taken on a national, not a local level. Local authorities, including National Park Authorities, were given the duty, this time enforced by Government and supported by a Government body, the Countryside Agency, to prepare detailed maps of Access Land. This was a contentious process with criteria having to be agreed and applied to specific areas of unenclosed upland, including common, open heath or woodland. Local Access Forums, with membership from a wide range of interest groups, were appointed and tasked both to oversee the process before maps of agreed areas were finally published, and to deal with issues arising from the management and usage of the areas in each National Park and in other areas of countryside.

CROW Act public access areas, as on the older 1949 Act Access Areas, are now carefully managed, with defined walking routes onto the Access land, and by-laws including restrictions on dogs and powers to close the areas concerned at times of fire risk, or when shooting is due to take place. Indeed it has been claimed that if anything the CROW Act may have restricted some walkers' informal freedoms, allowing closure at such times at short notice, and clearly reduces areas where dogs can be taken. But that is a minor quibble compared with having a clear indication, on maps, of land which is officially (usually) open to the walker, without fear of being turned off or threatened as a trespasser.

The majority of Open Access land is in the northern and western parts of England and Wales, much of it in National Parks and AONBs. Access land in the south is largely confined to much smaller areas of heath, downland and common, though there are important areas in the new South Downs National Park and in one of Britain's most significant areas of ancient common land, the New Forest now also a National Park. Such areas though generally smaller in overall area are equally important, given their accessibility to large numbers of people in the more densely populated areas of southern England. The Forestry Commission, ironically currently facing privitisation proposals, has also declared public access to its massive estates of woodland and forest throughout Britain.

Scotland however has always enjoyed a radically different tradition and legislative framework than England. Scottish walkers have enjoyed far greater rights of access over open country and forest for generations, being closer to other northern European countries. The Land Reform (Scotland) Act of 2003 consolidated much of Scottish access legislation, establishing freedom of access in Scotland, and specifying the rights and responsibilities of land managers, countryside users and recreational managers

Ironically, since the CROW Act in England and Wales was passed and implemented, there has not been a mad rush of "hordes" of ramblers heading for the peat hags and rushy bogs of the hills that many moorland managers feared. Typical usage is a couple of lone walkers following an already well defined track along a ridge, causing little or no disturbance to wildlife, sheep or grouse.

It could be argued that the huge machinery of state required to bring in and implement this powerful legislation for the relatively small minority even of committed walkers who want to escape to the wild places was not a cost effective use of resources, a large sledgehammer to crack a somewhat small nut. But that is to miss the point. The notices which once warned people threatening them (misleadingly) with prosecution for trespass if they walked a few metres across parts of the Bowland Fells of Lancashire, or to certain summits in the South Pennines, the Yorkshire Dales, North Pennines or North Wales have been consigned to the dustbin, as they have from many other areas of moorland and heathland in England and Wales. It was the simple knowledge that there was so much countryside from which people were denied access which was the real issue.

In some areas, such as the Yorkshire Dales, the CROW Act has made a huge difference. Until 2005 only 4% of the Yorkshire Dales National Park was open public access land. After 2005 this figure rocketed to 62%, a massive 390 square miles of open country where in theory at least you can wander at will on foot, freely and without hindrance or feelings of guilt.

Uniquely in England and Wales you now can buy a large scale Ordnance Survey map at any shop or tourist centre and see clear networks of legal footpath, bridleways and even permissive paths clearly marked in green on the 1:25,000 Explorer maps. From 2005 this has also included CROW Act Access Land, shaded in a light peach colour, so a walker can see at a glance just where he or she can freely and legally walk.

The Ordnance Survey do not have a monopoly of that information, and independent publishers such as Harvey Maps of Perthshire with their maps produced from aerial surveys, as well as hundreds of independent publishers and local authorities who produce countless maps and guidebooks now filling the shelves of every bookshop and Tourist Office, are witness to this explosion of interest and involvement in our footpath and countryside heritage.

It has been estimated that England alone contains over 188,000 kilometres – about 118,000 miles – of rights of way. The typical spider's web network of local footpaths, bridleways and byways (though byways are not always clearly indicated on current maps, generally being shown as "white roads"), readily available for the walker in most areas of England and Wales, represents a remarkable environmental asset, unique in Europe and indeed the world. It also has huge economic value – the Ramblers' Association have estimated that walkers contribute over £6 billion per year (at 2002 prices) to Britain's rural economy. Walking those paths also has profound implications, as we shall suggest later, for physical and mental health and well-being.

But above all footpaths connect us to our sometimes long-forgotten roots in the land, in the living past. No footpath exists by accident. Every footpath is there for a reason, a purpose, reflecting myriads of journey purposes, by people within communities whose lives have been shaped by the physical ability to enter and pass over that stretch of land.

It is an awesome piece of history, part of our identity, and rightly deserves the highest levels of protection. As we shall suggest, our footpath network is every bit as relevant and important to present and to future generations as it has been to the past.

5. LONG DISTANCE WALKING

A fool always wants to shorten space and time: a wise man wants to lengthen both – John Ruskin

Geoffrey Chaucer, author of *The Canterbury Tales*.

Walking long distances, over two or more days with overnight breaks at intermediate points, is a different kind of experience to a shorter day walk where you return home or to a holiday base.

A long distance walk is about discovering the true scale and complexity of the landscape, experiencing a sense of interlinking places. It's also about discovering something about yourself – relying on your own muscle power, your capacity of endurance, achieving longer distances step by step, stage by stage. When you walk a longer distance, the means of getting to that destination is as important as the destination itself, a goal in a personal as well as a physical sense. For most us, it is an achievement we are rightly proud of.

This is as true as it was for older forms of long distance walking, especially a pilgrimage on foot, where the purpose of the journey and the destination of the journey was as much spiritual as physical.

Since the dawn of history, men and women have been making pilgrimages, travelling sometimes very long distances to places of religious or spiritual significance. Pilgrimages to Jerusalem, Mecca, Rome, or the shrines of countless saints and holy men and women, have been part of the lives of many millions of people over countless generations. Most would be made on foot or horseback, and only in comparatively recent times by any form of mechanised transport. The humble pilgrim, with his cloak, staff and his scallop shell emblem, is a constant feature of medieval and renaissance art. Pilgrimage routes were developed and well established in medieval times, often with small wayside shrines and chapels to comfort and reassure travellers along the way. Even the Emperors and Tsars of Russia, including Empress Elizabeth (1709-1762), took the 70km pilgrimage walk between the palaces of Moscow and the Trinity Monastery of St Sergius, in Sergiyev Posad, followed by a caravan of waggons and retainers to offer the royal personage adequate rest and refreshment along the way.

To what extent these pilgrimages might be described as leisure journeys rather than purely utilitarian travel is a moot point. Some such as the pilgrimage to Santiago de Compostela in northern Spain, or to Santuario de Chimayó in New Mexico or Croagh Patrick in Ireland have kept much or all of their religious significance even to the present day.

But there is little doubt that in England, by the time of Geoffrey Chaucer, in the late 14th century, pilgrimages undertaken by groups of pilgrims were largely a social occasion. Companionship both on the road and overnight at the many inns and taverns catering for their refreshment and comfort was a highlight of many a pilgrimage.

Chaucer's masterpiece *The Canterbury Tales* wittily evokes how at the time of the "sweet showers" and warm sunshine of April,

Then people long to go on pilgrimages
And palmers long to seek the stranger strands
Of far-off saints, hallowed in sundry lands,
And specially, from every shire's ends
In England, down to Canterbury they wend

.

Clearly, as the magnificent selection of Tales reveals, these were social, pleasurable events. Though Chaucer's pilgrims being essentially the better-off classes, rode on horseback rather than walked.

There is some doubt as to whether or not the so-called Pilgrims' Way between Winchester and Canterbury along the North Downs was ever actually used by medieval pilgrims. Much of it uses ridge way tracks or generally runs along the spring line near the foot of the scarp faces of the Downs, linking villages. Such a high-level, meandering route would not have been attractive to medieval travellers in days before motor traffic. Most pilgrims, including Chaucer's, would have used the lower-level, less steeply graded main highways, with comforting inns for rest and refreshment at strategic intervals. In later centuries these became improved into toll-charging turnpike roads, and are now the modern arterial or trunk roads from London and other major centres. They include the former Roman road, Watling Street, now the A2, not exactly a pleasurable or safe place either to walk or to ride a horse in the 21st century. What is now shown as the Pilgrims' Way along the higher parts of the Downs was a name given to it by a somewhat fanciful Ordnance Survey cartographer in the mid 19th century. The error has been enshrined in later editions of OS maps and in common parlance ever since. Parts of this ersatz Pilgrims' Way are now incorporated in the modern North Downs Way.

Until relatively recent times most walkers covering long distances on foot across country, whether for business of pleasure, were happy to use the ordinary public highways for most or all of their journeys, as away from the larger towns, sharing a road with a relatively small number of carriages, waggons and horse riders along the King's Highway was not a problem.

The coming of motor vehicles, and faster straighter roads was to change all that. Even by the 1930s car traffic in Britain, though a miniscule two million cars on the roads compared with the 31 million of today, had reached a level where Professor Joad writing in 1933 could already grumble that road traffic was destroying both the walker's quality of experience and the countryside itself. As well as noting cars like "lines of ants"

The motoring age comes to the Yorkshire Dales – one of the first private cars in the Grassington area.

along the arterial roads, even country lanes were no longer sacred to walkers but suffered constant intrusions to the rambler's tranquillity and sense of security:

Shamelessly and incontinently, the motorist bears down upon you, driving you up the bank or into the hedge: insistently and relentlessly he sounds his horn in your ear. Men in particular can tolerate neither thing nor person on the road beside themselves, and sound their horn at sight. After a time the thing gets on one's nerves. One finds oneself starting at the least sound; perpetually one looks over one's shoulder wondering whether that is another loathed car come to break the spell of peace and solitude.

The answer to increasingly busy minor roads now no longer being either safe or pleasant for walkers, of course, was to make more use of off-road paths and tracks – the ancient and much neglected footpath, bridleway and byway network. But these rarely linked up to create a continuous network of walking routes. Even as late as the 1960s the writer, naturalist and walker John Hillaby (1917-96), undertaking his walk from Land's End to John O' Groats (becoming his best-selling *Journey Through Britain* published in 1968), could despair at finding enough linking tracks and paths without having to walk on tarmac:

I set off with the intention of avoiding all roads. I meant to keep to cross-country tracks and footpaths all the way. In places this turned out to be practically impossible for notwithstanding what's been written about the ancient by-ways, many of them are now hopelessly overgrown; others have been enclosed, ploughed up, or deliberately obstructed in one way or another. As far as I know you can't get into the Midlands from the Welsh border or cross the Lowlands of Scotland without making use of country lanes, derelict railway tracks or, in places, the towpaths of the old canals.

On a near-deserted road, three lady ramblers head away from Horton-in-Ribblesdale – heart of the Three Peaks country – in the late 1940s. By the 1970s it was impossible to walk any distance along public roads in safety, owing to the massive increase in car and lorry traffic.

– though old railway tracks and canals now in fact provide the basis of some of our most popular cross-country routes. But what was needed was the creation of sufficient off-road long distance waymarked footpaths or trails crossing Britain as envisaged in the 1949 National Park and Access to the Countryside Act. By the end of the 20th century this finally had begun to happen.

In fact creating and using long distance paths and trails for leisure walking had been established in many other countries on both sides of the Atlantic long before they came to Britain.

Germany is a country where walking or "Wanderung" is an integral part of the national culture, much more so than in Britain. Most German politicians, whether of the left, right or centre, feel it worthwhile to appear in walking gear on television or at public rallies to assert their closeness to their electorate. Fernwanderung, or long distance walking for leisure, dates back in Germany to the later 19th century.

The Black Forest Society was established in 1864 specifically to campaign for better walking trails through the Black Forest in south- west Germany. In 1900 the Society created what is perhaps the world's first purpose-made, fully waymarked long distance leisure walking trail with the opening of the Hohenweg, or high level route, which later became the Westweg (West Way) – a 203 km route between the town of Pforzheim to the north of the Black Forest in Baden-Wurtemburg, and Basle, Switzerland. The Mittelweg or Middle Way followed in 1903, the Ostweg or East Way soon afterwards in 1904.

Sweden was soon to follow with its own major long distance trail, with the 182 km Kungsleden in Lapland, north of the Arctic Circle, which was established before World War I and which remains one of Europe's most popular challenge hiking trails through wilderness countryside.

But it was the concept of the popular Black Forest trails in particular which were to cross the Atlantic

Typical Black Forest, Germany farmhouse close to the West Way, the first purpose-designed long-distance leisure walking route opened in 1900.

Black Forest footpath waymarking system, indicating a busy cross roads of long distance paths and linking routes.

when in 1909, James Paddock Taylor, a teacher from Vermont, who had enjoyed walking the trails in Germany, had an idea to develop a similar route through the Green Mountains of his native Vermont. He established the Green Mountain Club in Vermont in 1910. With a membership of 23 and just $100 in the bank, Taylor and his colleagues set about actually cutting the trail through the virgin forest. It took a full seven years to hack out the 265-mile route, known as the Long Trail, between the mountain peaks of Massachusetts and the Canadian Border. When completed the Long Trail had, as in the Black Forest, an additional network of 175 miles of side paths linking settlements and transport nodes with the mainline route.

This was followed by what became the most famous American long distance trail of all, the Appalachian Way. Again this was the inspiration of one individual, Benton MacKay, a philosopher and conservationist. In 1921 MacKay proposed a huge 2,100 mile route along the eastern part of the USA from Springer Mountain, Georgia, to Mount Katahadin in Maine. It was completed in 1937 as the world's longest continuous footpath, first "through walked" in 1948. It has simple shelters along the route to protect walkers from severe weather, and, a hazard absent from the UK at least, marauding bears. MacKay's original concept was for a route which linked camps where city dwellers could learn about the conservation of nature rather than through the non-stop walking trail it has now become. Though only around 100 sturdy hikers walk the entire route each year, an estimated 3-4 million people a year walk shorter sections of the Way.

The Appalachian Way led directly to the creation of Britain's first official long distance path. In 1935 two young British women who had spent a holiday walking part of the Appalachian Way wrote to Tom Stephenson, at that time a journalist with his regular outdoor column in the Daily Herald. Tom's response was to write what was to be a historic article "Wanted: A Long Green Trail" suggesting a similar trail be created along the Pennines of Northern England – a Pennine Way.

Tom's article created huge interest and the formation, in 1938, of the Pennine Way Association. The Association organised a conference in Hope, in the Peak District, which passed a resolution, part of which read:

The wide, health-giving, moorland and high places of solitude, the features of natural beauty and the places of historic interest along the Pennine Way give this route a special character and attractiveness which should be available for all time as a natural heritage for the youth of the country and of all who feel the call of the hills and the lonely places.

The Association went on to undertake a detailed survey of the proposed 250 mile route between Edale, Derbyshire through the Dark Peak, South Pennines, Yorkshire Dales, North Pennines and Cheviots to Kirk Yetholm on the Scottish Border. This established that no less than 70 miles of new footpath would be required to complete the Way, a formidable challenge.

When World War II intervened, it seemed that achieving Tom's vision would be an impossibility. Such an undertaking clearly would not be achieved without huge political support. This came about

Two walkers on a paved section of the Cleveland Way, opened in 1969. (Natural England - Tessa Bunney)

Tom Stephenson (left) stands next to Fred Willey MP as they launch the complete Pennine Way. The ceremony took place on Malham Moor in April 1965. (Yorkshire Post Newspapers)

Malham Moor was also the venue for the twentieth anniversary celebrations of the opening of the Pennine Way. The guests included Mike Harding (right), then President of the Ramblers' Association, who is seen here talking with Dr Arthur Raistrick. (G J Bosnyak)

through the Dower report of 1945 and the Hobhouse Committee on which Tom Stephenson was happily a member. The Hobhouse Committee in their 1947 Report suggested six long distance paths:

The Pennine Way.
The Ridgeway (from Cambridge to Seaton in Devon.)
The so-called Pilgrims Way from Winchester to Canterbury – (now included as part of the North Downs Way).
From Beachy Head along the South Downs to Winchester (the South Downs Way).
An Offa's Dyke Path.
A Teddington-Crickland Path along the Thames (now the Thames Path).

The Hobhouse Committee also suggested the creation of continuous lengths of footpaths around the coastlines of England and wales including each of the proposed new National Parks. This initially was to include the Pembrokeshire Coast Path, the Cleveland Way through the North York Moors and parts of what is now the South West Peninsular Coast Path along Exmoor.

The subsequent 1949 Act established the National Parks Commission (later to become the Countryside Commission) and gave the new body the task to prepare a report for the Minister on each of the proposed long distance routes along which the public should be enabled to make extensive journeys on foot or on horseback. It was envisaged that each route should for the whole or greater part of its length not pass along roads used by motor vehicles.

It was hardly surprising, given Tom Stephenson's involvement, that the first route to be selected was the Pennine Way. This was approved by the Minister on 16 July 1951. However it took a further 15 years of complicated and sometimes fraught negotiations before the many "missing links" along the route were completed, with some landowners holding out to the bitter end over granting rights of way over their land. The Water Boards owning the great moorland water catchment grounds of the high Pennines were amongst the most obdurate. There was even dissent among many ramblers about the Pennine Way going over Kinder Scout on the grounds that it would "desecrate" the remote wilderness of Kinder.

The full 267 mile (429km) route was finally launched on 24 April 1965 at a ceremony on Malham Moor in the Yorkshire Dales led by Fred Willey MP, who had been present on Tom Stephenson's 1948 Pennine Way walk and who was now the Minister of Land and Natural Resources. Tom himself was there to share the triumph plus a gathering of some 2,000 well-wishers, including ramblers from all over Britain.

It was a huge and important achievement, even though a couple of years later, John Hillaby, using the Pennine Way as part of his Land's End to John o' Groats walk as part of his *Journey Through Britain*, could note a lack of waymarking and grumble that the Ramblers' "sixpenny pamphlet" of the Pennine Way was curiously indefinite, if not downright misleading.

But gradually the whole of the route, funded 100% by the taxpayer, was brought up to standard and became, and remains, one of the most popular long distance walking routes in Britain, still a challenge of fitness and endurance.

The National Parks Commission also had powers to create accommodation along long distance paths. On the Pennine Way, two new purpose built Youth Hostels were provided to serve walkers at key points along the route – in the market town of Hawes in Wensleydale and at Malham. Very appropriately Malham Hostel was designed by Dower and is still known as the John Dower Hostel, being less than two miles from the village of Kirkby Malham, where Dower, at that time already an invalid, wrote his celebrated report.

Other long distance footpaths were to follow, including many of these as originally suggested in the Hobhouse Report. These included the Cleveland Way along the Cleveland Hills and the coast of the North York Moors National Park in 1969, the Pembrokeshire Coast Path in 1970,

Two walkers on the Pennine Way approach Penyghent.

Having climbed Penyghent, a walker enjoys the magnificent view over Ribblesdale.
(Yorkshire Post Newspapers]

A stile and view of the Wye Valley from Offa's Dyke Path, opened in 1971.

Offa's Dyke Path in 1971, South Downs Way in 1972, the Cornish Coast Path in 1972, the Ridgeway in 1973, the South Devon and Dorset Coast Paths in 1974, the Somerset & North Devon Coast Path in 1978, the North Downs Way in 1978, the Wolds Way (now the Yorkshire Wolds Way) in 1982 and the Peddars Way & Norfolk Coast Path in 1986.

The creation of these long distance paths was not without controversy. Many farmers and landowners fiercely resisted the creation of new paths and routes over their land, and sometimes long diversions along public roads had to be suffered until negotiations could be completed. This was the case with the Wolds Way, a 79-mile route through the largely agricultural landscapes of the Yorkshire Wolds. When the Countryside Commission decided to ask Lord Middleton, who had opposed the creation of sections of the proposed route on his land around the "lost" village of Wharram Percy, the East Riding Area of the Ramblers' Association were so offended – describing the Countryside Commission as "the landowners' poodle" – that they held their own opening ceremony on the same day on another part of the route. The Yorkshire Wolds Way as it is now known has recently been diverted to include the disputed sections.

Scotland, not being covered by the 1949 Act but enjoying its own footpath and access legislation (there being no equivalent of the English and Welsh Definitive Map), was slower to join the long distance trail revolution. But by 1980 the 95 mile West Highland Way from Mingrave, north of Glasgow, to Fort William had been opened, to be followed in 1981 by the Speyside Way from Spey Bay to Ballindalloch, being extended in stages to Tomintoul and Aviemore. The Southern Uplands Way between Portpatrick and Cockburnspath followed in 1984 and most recently the Great Glen Way in 2002. Northern Ireland has just one, albeit massive, 900km route, the Ulster Way which covers both coast and inland countryside.

The popularity and success of the new long distance trails took the official bodies by surprise. A detailed survey undertaken in 1990 suggested that around 10,000 people per annum were walking the "whole or a good part" of the Pennine Way between Edale and Kirk Yetholm. But a further 153,000 were walking shorter stretches of the route, making an estimated total 530,000 "walker days" along the Pennine Way and crucially (at 1990 prices) contributing about £2 million a year to the local rural economy. Significantly the highest percentage (56%) of this spending was by the 10,000 longer distance walkers who spent several nights staying in local accommodation along the route.

However, the cost and time of establishing new national long distance routes were becoming a serious worry to the Countryside Commission who had neither the finance nor the human resources to complete what was a long and complex process. User groups saw things differently – it was people, not bureaucrats that created paths.

It was in order to resolve this dilemma that the Commission in 1975 asked a retired accademic geographer Brunsdon Yapp to prepare a report on the future of long distance routes in England and Wales. Yapp developed the concept of national routes – i.e. routes of national importance that people would travel some distance to use, and regional routes, being important regionally and locally. This became the basis for the Commission's Policy Statement on Footpaths for Recreation, which encouraged local authorities to develop recreational strategies based on the planning and management of their footpath networks. At the same time it suggested there was a need for regional "Recreational Paths", which would be paths of major recreational value and importance supported by well maintained and promoted footpath networks.

This was a major step forward in that it recognised the intrinsic value of the historic footpath network for quiet outdoor recreation, and how local authorities could develop the network for the benefit of its citizens and indeed as a major rural tourism asset.

This concept was not universally welcomed by walkers however. Many members of the Ramblers' Association saw the development of footpath hierarchies as a means of "stealth rationalisation" by which certain footpaths would be well maintained and waymarked, but many others, especially where landowners and farmers didn't welcome their use, would be quietly neglected, left overgrown or blocked, and at some point in the future wiped off the map as no longer necessary for public use. Even though the Countryside Commission had promised to have "the entire right of way network to be legally defined, properly maintained and well publicised by the end of the century" (ie 2000) there was still concern that a too well planned network would focus on a series of popular walkways and see the greater footpath heritage neglected.

In fact the truth is somewhat between the two points of view. Inevitably, when resources are limited, local authorities have had to prioritise the networks which are promoted by themselves or other agencies and individuals in terms of footpath improvement, whilst at the same time ensuring that the less heavily used routes remain open, free from obstruction and signed and waymarked to at least minimum standards. But there are plenty of parts of mainly rural counties where footpaths maintenance is sadly neglected.

In 1989, when it was clear that the creation of long distance footpaths had slowed down to a snail's pace, a new policy was devised by the Countryside Commission for what were now called National Trails. This set out a hierarchy for the national network as a whole:

- National Trails – *routes of national importance through the finest areas of countryside. This might include certain routes which link to the European Long Distance Footpath network and be designated European Routes. The Trans Pennine Trail walking and cycling trail between Hull and Liverpool (E8) was the first E-Route to be designated, and has been followed by the E2 which take two "variant" routes between Harwich and Stranraer, and the E9 between Dover and Plymouth.*
- Regional Routes – *these would be paths of regional importance and include many of the suggested local authority sponsored recreational paths.*
- Local Paths – *this would include the well marked local networks for local and visitor leisure use.*
- Parish Paths – *paths into the "deeper countryside" but largely used by local people.*

From these deliberations, it was agreed that the Countryside Commission (from 1999 known as the Countryside Agency) would take forward proposals for a number of important additional National Trails – the Thames Path, Hadrian's Wall Path, the Cotswold Way and the Pennine Bridleway. The Pennine Bridleway is a spinal route along the Pennines for walkers, horse riders, and an important new and rapidly growing market, mountain bikers. It runs from Derbyshire eventually to Northumberland on a route parallel to the Pennine Way. It has popular loop paths – the Mary Townley Loop through the South Pennines, named after one of the keenest promoters of the Trail, Lady Mary Townley, and the Settle Loop across the high moorland above Malham in the Yorkshire Dales.

In addition to these new National Trails it was agreed to extend the South Downs Way through to Winchester. The new Countryside Council for Wales also took on board the development and promotion of the 120 mile Glyndwr's Way through the Welsh Marches and the mountains of central Wales.

Details of all the National Trails in England and Wales are now available on the National Trails website (www.nationaltrail.co.uk).

But even this is not the whole story. Not only did a mass of guidebooks to the new routes start to appear, but many local Areas and Groups of the Ramblers' Association began to research and publish their own suggestions for long distance routes. Since the 1970s, a huge number of official, semi-official and unofficial regional walking routes have become established by local authorities, by

A rest place and small maze on part the of York-Selby branch of the Trans-Pennine Trail, a walkers, cyclists and horse riders route across the Pennines, created by the cycle route charity Sustrans, which uses several sections of former railway lines. The Trans-Pennine Trail is now part of European long distance route E8, which crosses ten countries and currently ends at the Poland/Ukraine border.

Walkers cross Sandford Lock on the Thames Path. (Natural England - Anne Katrin Perkiss)

The Highway, an ancient moorland pass between Yorkshire and Cumbria, now carries the new Pennine Bridleway.

Area and Groups of the Ramblers' Association and by individual authors and enthusiasts. With the publication of the Definitive Maps in England and Wales, it was now possible to work out quite imaginative long distance routes using existing Definitive Footpaths, Bridleways, Byways and where necessary short stretches of minor road, canal towpath and old railway trackbed to cross very large areas of Britain.

Most local authorities now have their own locally sponsored and waymarked medium distance circular or linear recreational routes around or through the countryside, including through the Green Belts surrounding most larger towns and cities. Encouraged by the Countryside Agency and its successor, Natural England and the Countryside Council for Wales, and Scottish Natural Heritage in Scotland, countless new routes have been created to improve access to countryside on the edge of towns and cities, the so-called "countryside on the doorstep" of Britain's major urban areas.

Some routes initially sponsored by the Ramblers' Association such as the Thames Path and the Cotswold Way have now been officially recognised as National Trails. But others such as the Dales Way and the Coast to Coast Walk have failed to achieve national recognition, in both these cases because of the negative attitude of one local authority. In the late 1980s the Yorkshire Dales National Park Authority took the view at that time that there were "too many National Trails" through the Park. Ironically this hostility denied the both popular, nationally-known routes' potential additional national funding and resources which would have helped their maintenance and waymarking.

In the case of the 78 mile Dales Way from Ilkley to the Lake District (which also has direct links from the centres of Leeds, Bradford and Harrogate) the officially attitude changed dramatically in 2001/2 after the horrific social and economic impact of foot and mouth disease. This resulted in all footpaths and bridleways in the National Park being closed for well over a year with the loss of visitors' spending power. It was then realised that the 4,000 or so people a year walking the Dales Way, staying in local pubs and bed and breakfast establishments, buying meals, drinks and local souvenirs, made an immensely valuable contribution to the local economy along the route's corridor. One key aim of the voluntary Dales Way Association is to seek long overdue formal recognition of the Dales Way as a National Trail, which, in terms of the number of guide books published and numbers of people walking the route from all over the UK and from overseas, it truly is. Another is to work with local accommodation providers to help promote the route nationally and internationally as a very special way of experiencing the Yorkshire Dales and Lake District.

This has helped to create a new perspective within the National Park Authority which perceives long distance walking as exactly the kind of sustainable or green tourism that National Parks were set up to encourage. The Dales Way Association now works closely with the National Park Authority to promote and develop the route, but sadly without the benefit of national funding.

The Dales Way Association is only one of several specialist groups such as the Pennine Way, Offa's Dyke, the Icknield Way and the Cotswold Way Associations that effectively campaign to support and promote their particular long distance route.

Even more surprising is the fact that Wainwright's 190 mile long Coast to Coast Walk is not officially a National Trail in spite of it being probably Britain's most popular long distance walking route, again one that is widely known nationally and internationally, and frequently promoted on national television.

The Coast to Coast Walk owes its existence purely to one individual who has become an icon of the long distance walking movement in Britain – W.A. (Alfred) Wainwright (1907 - 1991). Wainwright was a Blackburn local government officer and hill walker who, in his spare time and into his retirement, produced a series of magnificently drawn and handwritten "pictorial guides" to the Lakeland Fells from the 1950s onwards. For a generation these have been essential handbooks to anyone walking in the Lake District, and with his Howgills and Limestone Country Guides, to the Yorkshire Dales. He also published a superb *Pennine Way Companion* whose detailed maps and line drawings avoid all the problems of routes finding suffered by John Hillaby. However, it is his *Coast to Coast Walk* that describes his own route from St Bees on the Cumbria Coast to Robin Hood's Bay in North Yorkshire, across the Lake District, Yorkshire Dales and North York Moors National Parks, that has captured the public imagination. He describes the route in meticulous detail but with his usual dry humour. Towns and villages along the Walk have all benefited enormously from the tens of thousands of modern pilgrims in the footsteps of the master.

Inevitably there have been lots of Wainwright imitators, writers and cartographers who have attempted to produce the same kind of meticulous hand drawn maps and drawings to illustrate walks. Some, such as the late Arthur Gemmell of Otley and Paul Hannon of Keighley, are very good indeed. But none have quite captured that Wainwright magic, that crusty, eccentric yet delightful personality which makes the books so compelling and which have created such an interest and enthusiasm for long distance as well as for more local walking. Not surprisingly, there is a Wainwright Society dedicated to perpetuate the memory and achievement of the artist and writer. Even more importantly perhaps, the Society is currently updating the famous guides for a new generation of readers.

W A (Alfred) Wainwright, 1907 - 1991.

Walker on the Dales Way near Grandsire, Crook.

Group of walkers following the Dales Way in Lunesdale.

Julia Bradbury on Wainwright's Coast to Coast Walk. (Skyworks)

Elaine's Teas – farmhouse teas and comfort on the Coast to Coast Walk near Marske, Swaledale.

But long distance walking has also created its own small but booming industry, both in terms of the companies which have now emerged to provide tailor-made transport of baggage in vans and minibuses and also support and rescue for walkers along Britain's most popular trails. There's also a huge publishing industry with literally hundreds of walker-writers now producing their own carefully researched guidebooks to a medium or long distance trail they have devised. Some, such as Mark Reid's Inn Way series, have a tie up with local accommodation providers, in Mark's case country inns which offer a special welcome to walkers. Others, such as Skyware of Saltaire, Bradford, are both writers and publishers, combining cartographical, writing and publishing skills in launching their 90 mile Dales Highway between Saltaire and Appleby.

Some routes only last as long as their authors' books are in print, doomed to drift into obscurity. Others have become popular, well established routes, eventually achieving the ultimate accolade, inclusion on the Outdoor Leisure Ordnance Survey Maps, to be marked with the little green diamonds that indicate an established National Trail or Regional Recreational Path. Most of these routes now link up with other routes, so if you have the time and inclination, you can now truly cross England and Wales, and much of Scotland, by marked trails, picking up one key long distance route to link with another.

Establishing such an informal network has been a truly magnificent achievement. Even more interesting is the fact that it has largely happened in an unplanned way and uncoordinated way, as the result of individual enthusiasms and passion for walking. It is truly a Peoples' Network.

The body that co-ordinates all such information on both the official and unofficial long distance walks in the UK is the Long Distance Walkers' Association (ldwa.org.uk) which every few years re-issues *The UK Trail Walkers Handbook*. This provides a database of all known British local long distance walks (over 700 at last count, covering more than 40,000 trail miles) – an unofficial but authoritative Doomsday Book which gives status and recognition to any properly researched and well documented long distance footpath route in Britain that meets the LDWA's criteria for inclusion. The Association also has 42 local branches, which organise regular group events, including Challenge walks for their members and affiliated groups (a "Challenge" walk is defined as anything between 20 and 100 miles). Certificates are issued for people who have completed at least five National Trails or Scottish Long Distance Routes or personal records kept of other hill walking feats or trails that have been "bagged". The excellent web site not only allows walkers to source each and every one of the paths, and their supporting websites and publications, but also locates them on Ordnance Survey maps. The webmasters are in the process of developing a superb interactive base of accommodation so that a trail-finder can not only find where to walk and stay but even book that crucial overnight accommodation – a real boost to rural economies.

The LDWA can be seen as providing opportunity for more strenuous walking activity which lies at one end of the spectrum of leisure walking, reflecting a long tradition of walking as an energetic, even competitive, sport dating back to the mighty physical challenges and pedestrian feats of the 18th and 19th centuries.

At the other end of that spectrum is what we have defined as "gentle walking", which involves taking perhaps a good deal longer to cover at least some of those distances, yet offering a different, but equally rewarding, walking experience.

Long distance walking over several days at whatever speed you travel offers perhaps the purest form of walking. You are totally dependent on your own feet and muscles for perhaps several days at a time, not reliant on a car or bus at the end of the day. By staying overnight you spend more time and money within a local community and share a sense of place with companions or anyone you happen to meet. To start out on a day's walk in the morning from somewhere away from the familiar surroundings of home with a full day's walk ahead is also a worthwhile and rather special experience. There is also the advantage that without having to travel out to your starting point, you can begin your day's walk early and cover a greater distance by late afternoon or evening.

At the end of his walk from Land's End to John O' Groats, John Hillaby reflects on what makes long distance walking such a very special kind of experience:

Roads are all more or less alike. Walking is intimate; it releases something unknown in any other form of travel and, arduous as it can be, the spring of ground underfoot varies as much as the moods of the sky. By walking the whole way I got a sense of gradual transition from one place to another, a feeling of unity. The mosaic of my own country and its people had become a sensible pattern...

It is interesting to reflect had Hillaby been doing that same long distance walk through Britain in 2011 that he did in 1967, traffic might have been worse even on the minor roads and by-roads, but escaping those roads to walk northwards on a network of traffic free, well-waymarked National Trails or Regional Recreational Routes or Peoples' Paths, would have been much easier, indeed perfectly possible thanks to the work of the LDWA and individual Ramblers groups and other bodies.

Long distance walking in Britain received another major boost in November 2009 – more than 60 years after the wartime Scott Committee suggestion and Hobhouse Committee recommendation – when the Marine and Coastal Access Act became law, and with it proposals to create a continuous 2,500 mile long distance National Trail path around the whole of the English coast. This will require the creation of access on foot to the 50% of the English coastline that currently has no legal access, and will also absorb existing Trails such as the South West Coastal Path. Similar measures are anticipated in the future for Wales, where work has already started, and for Scotland.

This coastal path may take many years to be achieved by Natural England and its partners, especially as Britain enters a period of perhaps savage public expenditure cuts, though 2020 still remains the somewhat optimistic target for completion. But even if it is only created in stages, the new Coastal Path will create superb new opportunities for long distance coastal walking. Such opportunities are of special relevance for the inhabitants of and visitors to an island whose landscapes and seascapes along its huge and varied coastline are among its most priceless assets.

Few long-distance trails epitomise the glory of walking through stunning cliff scenery better than the Cornish section of the South West Coastal Path. These views reflect the striking contrasts, whether it be the near white sand, memorable sunsets, old engine houses from the days of tin mining or even cattle approaching on the path! Small wonder that there is eagerness to create a National Trail around the whole of the English coast. (photos: David Joy)

6. URBAN WALKING – RECLAIMING OUR CITIES

In great cities, spaces as well as places are designed and built: walking, witnessing, being in public, are as much part of the design and purpose as is being inside to eat, sleep, make shoes or love or music – Rebecca Solnit

There is only one way to discover a town or city centre and that is on foot. Only by walking the streets, squares, piazzas, boulevards are you able to enjoy the atmosphere, the architecture, the life of a city. But it's often away from the busy boulevards, office blocks and shopping malls that a real city is to be discovered – in the quieter side streets with their old inns or pavement cafes, in the courtyards and alleyways, where a city becomes alive and reveals its true character and meaning.

This is not only true of the famous cities of Europe – Vienna, Rome, London, Edinburgh, Paris, Prague, Budapest – but of almost any smaller town and city you can name.

The older and more historic the town, the less likely it is to have been destroyed, if not by wartime bombs, by the highway engineers and property developers.

Venice is one of the most gloriously beautiful towns on earth, but one of its unique qualities is that the historic city centre is totally car free – a true pedestrian and gondola city. The joy of Venice is to be found not just in the great showpiece Piazza of St Marco or by the Grand Canal, but the countless narrow streets, passageways and walkways that form an intricate labyrinth as they weave their way between the canals and great squares, at every turn revealing architecture of glorious if decaying splendour.

Or there is the great medieval city of Cordoba in southern Spain, which had a population of over a million in the tenth century, and which has retained its countless narrow alleyways and foot streets, with shops, palaces and tiny, vivid courtyard gardens, around the great Mezquita Mosque-Cathedral.

Such magnificent cities owe much to the fact that they were built and have evolved on a scale to meet the needs of the pedestrian, as indeed did most medieval, Renaissance, and even Georgian cities, even though by the 18th century grand carriageways for emperors and princes were replacing the human scale of walkways and foot streets.

But even the hugely developed, redeveloped and expanded and industrialised (and de-industrialised) towns and cities of Britain have retained their ancient hearts. Every city has an economic or political reason for its existence, which is reflected in its location. Economic origins may lie in the fact that it is a major port or harbour, the key crossing point of a river, or (frequently) the highest navigable point on a river where in a pre-railway age goods were brought by packhorse or canal and were traded or stored in warehouses before onward shipment by boat or horse-drawn waggon or packhorse train.

Political origins are usually linked to a castle or fortification, guarding a key trading route or strategic pass through the hill country. In Britain such towns are usually Norman or even Roman in origin, the great castle still a focal point, and close by parish church or cathedral, down from which runs a still busy high street, the home of traders and merchants that serviced the garrison, often the market place. Around this core, the "caer", "burgh" or fortified township grew, often originally protected by walls from human foes or even marauding wolves. The sites of medieval "burgess' houses with their dividing plots of "toft and crofts" and intervening alleyways and courtyards are still decipherable behind the modern shopping streets, and can still be explored on foot.

Many of our larger, industrialised towns retain

their ancient hearts, huddles of courtyards and alleyways where the city began. Edinburgh's medieval "Auld Reekie" is perhaps the most famous, but there is much to explore on foot around Bristol's old port area, Manchester's Shudehill, Leeds' Briggate and Calls, Nottingham's caves and castle, Birmingham's Gas Street Basin huddle of canal junctions and workshops.

Most modern cities are in fact agglomerations of old villages gradually swallowed up as the city expanded from its original kernel, their names now recorded as district neighbourhoods, yet still with a village atmosphere, the original winding main street often pedestrianised as a local shopping area, even village greens preserved as a small local park, old lanes fossilised as back alleys.

These are things the walker discovers, perhaps armed not just with the OS Outdoor Leisure Map, but the local A-Z where street names are often a delightful clue to what places once were in their rural past – Water Lane, Brook Street, Wool Pack Lane, Angel Meadow, Swinegate, streets often taking their name from sometimes long forgotten old taverns. As a general guide anything called "lane", "brow" or "yard" is likely to be old. Anything in the north of England known as "Gate" is undoubtedly ancient. "Gate" is derived from the old Norse word "gata" meaning a street or road. Even the suffix "Street" or "Road" is likely to indicate an origin no later than the 18th or 19th century.

Actual street names often give insight into the age and origin of a thoroughfare, from the more earthy medieval and Tudor – "Grape Lane" for example being a corruption of "Grope" referring to a village back lane frequented by lovers – to the more formal Georgian terraced boulevards named after monarchs and battles. Victorian streets are more typically named after outposts of the growing Empire, the children and siblings of the current monarch, or of a local worthy, whilst the blander, faux-rural names of 20th century suburbia – the Meadow Views, Orchard Avenues or Woodlands Crescents when there is no meadow, orchard or woodland anywhere in sight – are simply marketing a non-existent or long vanished rural idyll.

London is a rich treasure house of old ways and ancient names. Writers such as Samuel Johnson, the great essayist and first creator of the English Dictionary, was reputed to know every street, alleyway and tavern of his beloved London. Charles Dickens allegedly walked between 10 and 15 miles every day of his life, often through and around the narrow streets and courts of the older parts of central London. In daylight and at night, he soaked in the atmosphere and rich complexity of human settlement, history and habitation and behaviour that became the inspiration for many of his greatest novels, none more compelling than the fog-choked, corruption-ridden city that is almost the central character of Bleak House.

Not only do many more people still walk in central London for utilitarian reasons (it is often quicker and cheaper to walk from a station to the office or shop than use the Underground, bus or taxi network), but London has also long been recognised as a fascinating place for the urban walker. The city's rich patterns of old village settlements are not entirely lost under the massive later urban sprawl. Village layouts can still be discovered even within the teeming central as well as the commuter suburbs, with a village church, old pub, vicarage within a few hundred yards of the Underground station. Thanks to the constant vigilance of the Commons Society and others, precious green spaces – old village greens, parks, playing fields, cemeteries – can be linked by the walker using fragments of former rural paths and tracks, which against all the odds have survived, to make attractive cross city routes.

Not surprisingly most towns and cities of Britain now have their heritage trails or self-guided walking tours through their centres where the visitor can trace out the older township. But walking from city centres through suburbs and out into the nearby open countryside is more difficult to achieve – and not just because of the overall scale of industrial and residential development. Specific transport infrastructure, especially over the last century and a half, has created sometimes formidable barriers for the walker around the outskirts of towns and cities.

Victorian railways had a huge, often devastating, impact on many historic town and city centres. They were too often built by brilliant if single minded railway engineers in defiance of the historic patterns of the town, demolishing whole areas, actions which would have produced wholesale condemnation and defiance from today's conservationists and civic protection bodies such as English Heritage and Civic Trusts. In the case of York even the historic city walls were breached for the city's first station, whilst Newcastle lost part of its historic castle. High brick viaducts were constructed across the centres of towns demolishing anything in their path, even digging up graveyards and disinterring corpses to make way for the iron road. But that was not all. Railways brought with them their own massive development in the form of new stations, goods yards and carriage sidings, warehouses, station hotels and offices. Many of these areas have now been redeveloped for offices, retail outlets and even urban apartments, but the pattern of that development is still clear on the ground.

In Venice, canalside walkways link restaurants and shops with residential areas. With its intricate network of narrow foot streets and canals, central Venice is one of the most pedestrian friendly, traffic-free cities in Europe.

Opposite: Medieval foot street, Dubrovnik – a compact walled city that evolved for pedestrian and not vehicular use.

The impact of railways was trivial compared with that of road traffic and highways engineering of later generations. Over the last half century, catering for the car and truck has massively changed the character of most of our towns and cities, and in so doing has severely impacted on the quality of environment and has reduced opportunities for pedestrians.

Vehicular traffic now blights most town and city

centres, away from the relatively limited central pedestrianised zones. The sheer volume of vehicles stopping and starting along any busy city street, with noise, fumes and constant fear of injury, has turned many city centres into a living hell for walkers. Roads are often difficult and dangerous to cross, requiring long waits for a pause in the traffic or long diversion to a safe crossing point, therefore slowing down a cross-city walk. This is especially the case when highway engineers have "improved" certain city centre roads into designated one-way fast-flow loops, with traffic signals carefully calibrated to maximise traffic flows and reducing pedestrian access, with intrusive, motorway-style signing. Pedestrians are often corralled inside metal railings, forced into unpleasant, and often threatening underground passages (evocatively described by one commentator as "people-sewers") or held back by pelican crossings – often with dummy buttons to allow pedestrians to believe they have at least some control of the situation. Lights are deliberately timed to maximise traffic speeds and flows by restricting pedestrian crossing time and availability. This discriminates against anyone with a physical disability. You have to be physically fit to walk across many modern British city centres.

Highway engineers will, with some justification, suggest that such inner loops or ring ways are necessary to allow the creation of pedestrian areas within the city centres, by diverting through traffic away from the pedestrian zones. It is an attractive, if seductive thesis.

The concept of separating pedestrians and motorists (cyclists are a little more difficult to deal with) goes back to the highly influential report Traffic in Towns by Sir Colin Buchanan, published in 1963. The report warned:

It is impossible to spend any time on the study of the future of traffic in towns without at once being appalled by the magnitude of the emergency that is coming upon us. We are nourishing at immense cost a monster of great potential destructiveness [the motor vehicle], and yet we love him dearly.

Among solutions suggested by Buchanan were not only the physical separation of pedestrians and traffic, if necessary building new walkways above the traffic levels, but also banning cars from certain parts of towns, building underground car parks, having stricter parking controls and even a "congestion tax" on car owners.

Inevitably successive generations of planners and engineers have taken on board some effective solutions first suggested by Buchanan, such as better parking controls and central pedestrian areas. Birmingham has an excellent example of an elevated walkway that links New Street with the International Exhibition Centre through attractive piazzas of fountains and sculpture, giving the city, once infamous for its notorious Bull Ring traffic interchange, a much more European mainland feel. Other linking pedestrian streets in the city have followed.

Pedestrian zones as such were pioneered in a number of cities such as Coventry and Leeds during the 1960s. The initial proposals to close off Briggate and a few other streets in central Leeds produced huge initial opposition from traders who threatened to move out of the city, but proved hugely popular with the public. Within a few weeks city centre shopkeepers actually noticed increased "footfall" as people, not cars, came past their windows and into their shops, resulting in higher turnover. The opposition, except for a few diehard cases, rapidly disappeared, and over the next few decades the pedestrian areas expanded to cover much of the city centre.

But there was a trade off. This was the construction in Leeds of a new fast segregated Inner Ring Road, an Expressway, tunnelling under part of the city, from which pedestrians and cyclists were banned, and later an inner city Loop Road on using city roads immediately around the pedestrian area, with up to four lanes of fast traffic off the motorways roaring around the city centre along a racetrack, with few safe places to cross. The experience has been repeated in many other city centres such as Stafford or Lancaster – an attractive car-free kernel, accessible by car and public transport, but this area is tightly boxed in by often ferocious,

heavily congested loop roads and radial highways which are difficult and dangerous for pedestrians and cyclists to penetrate or to cross, and which inflict serious noise and air pollution on nearby properties.

Buchanan's other radical proposal for a congestion charge to reduce traffic congestion took a little longer to be achieved – about 40 years – and then in only one city in the UK. It took the charismatic and controversial Ken Livingstone to have Britain's only congestion tax scheme in central London. So far all other British cities have resoundingly rejected any suggestion of congestion charges. Referenda on proposals in both Edinburgh and Manchester for a congestion charge on peak hour

Over London by Rail. From the mid 19th century onwards railways began to dominate larger towns and cities, splitting communities and even overshadowing residential property. This engraving by Gustave Dore shows rows of houses dominated by London's new railway arches. Urban motorways were to do the same in the 20th century, reducing pedestrian freedom even more effectively.

Above: Cars, barriers and signs dominate many town centres, as seen here in Stockport, Greater Manchester.

Right: The other face of Stockport, where a pedestrianised street has allowed shoppers and strollers to reclaim part of the town centre.

Traffic lanes and urban motorways have come to dominate many a city – and often have few places for pedestrians to cross. (Campaign for Better Transport – 3)

Place de l'Homme de Fer, Strasbourg – the walker-friendly street tramway interchange giving access on foot to the pedestrianised city centre.

Nottingham Express Transit has proved a huge success in getting people out of their cars and encouraging them to walk in and around the city. (Campaign for Better Transport) motorists to fund huge public transport and pedestrian improvements were predictably defeated by a huge margin. Motorists won't give up their right to sit in a traffic jam and destroy their own and everyone else's environment so easily. But then the one place you are least aware of the environmental destruction caused by the car is sitting in a car.

Unlike Continental cities, most British cities have ignored suggestions to reduce loss of precious city centre land sacrificed to car parking by putting major car parks underground. Such car parks cost more money to build and motorists do not like them. So instead there are ever larger multi-storey car park blocks within or close to most city centres. Worst of all are the huge ground level car parking lots which effectively sterilise valuable land over a very significant part of most UK towns and cities.

The new city centre car parks in turn must be served by widened and heavily improved main radial roads into city centres from the suburbs, linked into the network of huge Outer and Inner Ring Roads to "distribute" the traffic into different parts of the city. Historic towns are often little more than large traffic islands imprisoned within heavily congested and polluted inner ring and distributor roads, which are difficult to cross on foot.

Naturally all such routes quickly gridlock with traffic in the ever extending morning and afternoon peaks, with urban air quality now a major threat to physical health, as the toxic combination of pollutants from both petrol and diesel engines contribute to a range of respiratory and other conditions including heart disease and cancers. It is a major public health problem, which even with proposed electric cars, will take generations to eradicate.

The growing problems of city centre traffic congestion have had two perhaps unexpected effects. They have given huge boost to urban rail travel – the Victorian suburban railways, unlike buses, are not victims of gridlock. But in a less welcome impact – and a serious failure of land use planning in Britain – it has also has encouraged the massive development of out-of-town car-accessible retail, business and even leisure centres. These are usually situated close to the outer ring roads and motorways, often close to motorway interchanges and simply identified as being at Junction 31 or wherever in the new language of the motorway culture. They all require massive new parking areas which, landscape blight apart, seriously disadvantage the non car-using pedestrian.

Even where good public transport exists, such out-of-town shopping facilities are usually far less convenient than town centre or neighbourhood facilities for people on foot, as unless it is on an inward bus route, most trips to such centres require two journeys by train or bus, the first into the town centre, the second back out to the retail park, a journey perhaps taking four times as long as by car, again powerfully reinforcing the car culture. If you don't drive you are effectively excluded from many shopping and leisure complexes including those now containing multiplex cinemas. In some towns and cities it is now difficult even to go to the cinema without a car.

Such major motorway served sub-regional Retail Centres as Meadowhall in South Yorkshire, the Metro Centre in Tyneside, Trafford Centre near Manchester, Merry Hill in the West Midlands and Lakeside in Essex have become cities-outside-the-city, with as many shops and facilities as a typical city centre, drawing in huge amounts of traffic, but also taking trade away from shops in the older city centres or once prosperous market towns.

Even when a new more human scale retail or leisure complex is built within the city suburbs, there is still a problem for anyone arriving on foot. Access generally requires a long walk from the nearest bus stop, across busy access roads filled with cars or trucks, through car parking areas, usually with no pavement and poor signage. This can create a bleak and forbidding environment especially in the hours of darkness.

So what has this to do with walking? Simply this. In many outer-urban areas of Britain, we have now created huge pedestrian-hostile areas where the physical barriers of huge new roads and parking lots, generally with little or no pedestrian access, are dangerous, unpleasant and threatening. These are no-go areas for pedestrians. Walkers are simply not welcome.

The American science fiction writer Ray Bradbury in his satirical story Twice 22, written as long ago as 1966 (the car culture became dominant a couple of decades earlier in USA than in the UK), illustrated the growing perception of the urban walker as somehow abnormal because he is not in the safe cocoon of his car. Set in a mythical Los Angeles in AD 2052, Bradbury's hero, Leonard Mead, a writer, is seen walking along a street and is duly arrested by an officer in a passing patrol car.

When Mead explains he was just "Walking for air – Walking to see", the interrogating cop asks him what is wrong with his home air conditioning and TV viewing screen, before arresting him and transporting him to the "Psychiatric Center for Research on Regressive Tendencies".

In fact, as another American, the historian and philosopher Lewis Mumford has suggested, walking is an extremely efficient form of transportation for short distance, especially in a city environment. It is infinitely more efficient than the automobile in terms of usage of space available. Indeed in most city centres, at peak times it is quicker to walk a couple of miles than take a bus or taxi. The huge numbers of walkers in London, say crossing Waterloo Bridge at rush hour, bears this out.

Nearly half a century ago, in 1963, Mumford was suggesting that urban planners and highway engineers need to treat the urban walker in very a different way:

Every urban transportation plan should, accordingly, put the pedestrian at the centre of all its proposals, if only to facilitate wheeled traffic. But to bring the pedestrian back into the picture, one must treat him with the respect and honor we now accord only to the automobile. We should provide him with pleasant walks, insulated from traffic, to take him to his destination, once he enters a business precinct or residential quarter....

.....Why should anyone have to take a car and drive a couple of miles to get a package of cigarettes or a loaf of bread, as one must do in a suburb? Why, on the other hand, should a growing minority of people not be able to again walk to work, by living in the interior of the city, or for that matter, be able to walk home from the theatre or the concert hall?

Rather than being a nuisance or a problem to be tolerated ("vulnerable road user" is the official description by highway engineers for a pedestrian), walkers should therefore be centre stage in any urban transport planning proposals.

But it is not all bad news. For over 80 years there has been one UK organisation actively campaigning for the rights of the walker in the urban environment – the Pedestrians' Association, founded in 1929, and now known as Living Streets. It has successfully campaigned for 20mph speed limits on some urban residential streets, which it would like to see imposed on all residential streets. This is supported by massive evidence of the saving of life and serious injury accidents this would achieve. It would also like to see a dramatic improvement in the management of the street environment so that the needs of local residents and walkers are put ahead of those of the motorists or rat-running commuters. Living Streets points to experience in the Netherlands where Woonerf or Home Zones have used street furniture and chicanes, including tree and shrub plantings, to eliminate such hazards as speeding traffic, illegal or thoughtless parking on pavements, so that children can play in and ramblers can walk through residential areas of cities without feeling threatened. A current key Living Streets project is for "Naked Streets" where shared space for cars, cyclists and wheelchair users can allow all different travel activities to take place in a non threatening environment.

Clearly, creating local streets which are pleasant and safe to walk through is of huge benefit to walkers, cyclists and local communities alike. They can go a long way to helping to reduce the

An out-of-town shopping centre close to a city ring road. Such retail developments are planned around unrestricted use of the private car with free parking and thus require huge areas of land. They are far less convenient for pedestrians than traditional town or suburban high street shops.

problems of car dependency by creating a greener, more attractive alternative way of travel. Fear of traffic is, paradoxically, a major cause of traffic generation as people drive themselves and their children in the perceived "safety" of their vehicle rather than walk, cycle or take the bus, which requires a perceived "risky" walk to the bus stop.

The American writer Rebecca Solnit, in her fascinating study of the history and politics of walking, *Wanderlust*, rightly identifies the loss of freedom to walk safely in a town or city, free from physical or sexual harassment, as a key feminist issue. Streets busy with pedestrians are safe streets – lonely, isolated car-dominated streets and malls are where women typically suffer male violence, discrimination and stereotypical attitudes.

A related dimension is a city's designated open spaces. The larger the town or city, the more important are its open spaces. Gradually there is growing recognition of the massive contribution that has been made in the past, and will be made in the future, by Britain's urban parks. It's not just

The promenade in People's Park, Halifax, laid out by Joseph Paxton, the builder of the Crystal Palace. This photograph dates from about 1900.

a question of dog walkers (though walking the dog is perhaps the single most important incentive for people to walk in the urban environment), but for the health of the whole community, where again people of all ages and both genders can walk, stroll and feel safe.

Parks for urban people is a relatively new phenomenon, a result of the great post-Peterloo reforming zeal that also helped safeguard rural commons and open spaces. In 1833, just a year after the great Reform Act, the Select Committee on Public Walks was recommending that voluntary bodies, local and central Government should fund open "green" spaces in or near areas where working people lived to offer fresh air and exercise.

The first such public park, the 200 acre Victoria Park in East London was opened in 1845, and it is reported that within a few months over 20,000 people were making use of the new park on a single day. London's eight Royal Parks whilst still technically belonging to the Crown, have since 1851 effectively been public parks, managed with other open spaces in London by the Royal Parks Agency.

Other public parks soon followed in industrial towns and cities outside London. One of the most iconic was Birkenhead Park, across the Mersey from Liverpool, which was opened in 1847 to the design of Joseph Paxton, who was later to create the Crystal Palace. Paxton's designs were much admired by the American landscape architect Frederick Law Olsted, who incorporated many of its key features in his design for Central Park, New York. Paxton also designed the aptly named 12½ acre People's Park, in Halifax, which was purchased by the local carpet manufacturer Sir Francis Crossley and opened in 1857 for the people of Halifax "for all time."

In Liverpool, Newsham, Stanley and Sefton parks were opened between 1868 and 1872. Birmingham's Aston Park was purchased for the city with help from a local philanthropist in 1874. Roundhay Park Estate in Leeds, at that time well outside the built-up area of the city, was purchased

Heaton Park, Manchester – a magnificent area of parkland and landscape gardens on the outskirts of the city.

Roundhay Park, Leeds. (F.M. Penford)

in 1871 thanks to the vision of the then Mayor of Leeds, John Barron. The Mayor and his colleagues purchased the estate, for the huge sum, at that time, of £139,000 to secure it, and then sold it back to the City of Leeds for the same price – an Act of Parliament was required to enable this to be done. With its 700 acres – 2.8 square kilometres – it is one of the largest city parks in Europe, and is now enjoyed by over a million visitors annually. Again showing its remarkable vision, in 1891 the City Council opened the world's first overhead trolley electric tram service from the city centre to allow the people of Leeds to make the three-mile journey to the Park. Sadly, the tram service was discontinued in the 1950s.

Manchester's fine 650 acre Heaton Park, just four miles from the city entre, was purchased by Manchester Corporation from the Earl of Wilton in 1902. This included Heaton Hall, an 18th century listed building, with its extensive gardens and parkland. Like Roundhay Park, Heaton Hall was also served by the city's tramway system, and is now happily accessible by a station on the city's modern Metrolink light rail network. A short stretch of the original tramway, complete with historic trams, now runs inside the Park. Not only does the Park offer splendid walks on the edge of the city, but there are linking paths along the Irwell Valley Way, with sections of quiet road, that allow Heaton Park to be reached from the city centre on foot.

Glasgow is another city extremely well served with public parks, with over 90 parks and formal gardens within its boundaries, whilst Liverpool has over 70. Birmingham's Sutton Park covers no less than 2,400 acres of woodland heath and wetlands, and has recently been designated a National Nature Reserve – and yet is only six miles from the city centre.

Other towns and cities have been fortunate in keeping some immense green spaces protected as ancient commons. London's Royal Parks, Hampstead Heath and Epping Forest have already been mentioned but Newcastle still enjoys the benefits of its superb Town Moor, whilst the remnants of the ancient Forest of Knaresborough remained unenclosed in the 1770s in Harrogate to allow public access to the chalybeate and sulphur wells – superb areas of open grassland known as The Stray. York also has a number of open areas of commons or Strays outside the ancient walled city which now provide valuable green lungs and walking spaces especially as these link with old footpaths and more modern cycle ways into the city centre.

There is a growing recognition that the great Victorian parks of our cities and towns, too often neglected over the last century or so, represent immensely important, easily accessible, green lungs for future generations. They are wonderful areas within which to walk for an hour or so of healthy exercise in green surroundings given their relative ease of access on foot and by public transport from huge centres of population. Most British towns and cities have major projects to restore and rediscover their Parks, both as neighbourhood facilities for local communities and also as major tourist attractions in their own right for visitors to their towns.

But there is another key element of parks, gardens, playing fields and even churchyards and cemeteries, and that is their role as part of linear urban walking routes.

Sheffield and Leeds are examples of cities with huge potential for walking within their boundaries in that they share a geographic position on the eastern slopes and foothills of the Pennines which has prevented parts of the two cities from being as intensively developed as more low lying cities such as Liverpool and Manchester. Sheffield actually includes part of the Peak District National Park, whilst Leeds lies on the lower slopes of two Yorkshire dales – Airedale and Wharfedale. Sheffield claims with some justification to be one of the greenest cities of Europe, with no less than 3,885 hectares of park or open space within its boundaries. You can walk from the city centre through Eccleshall and Abbeydale Woods or along the Loxley Valley into the Peak National Park. Leeds has one special narrow, undeveloped, typical steep Pennine oak and birch wood gill, a tributary of the Aire, the Meanwood Valley, a remarkable green corridor through the north west city suburbs. You can walk from Woodhouse Moor close to the city centre, through typical Victorian alleyways or "ginnels" of Headingley past gardens and allotments, via Woodhouse Ridge, Meanwood Park, Adel Wood, Eccup and Bramhope and Otley into Wharfedale – the Dales Way Leeds Link to Ilkley Moor and Ilkley, continuing through the Yorkshire Dales onto Bowness on Windermere.

You can even walk out of central Manchester towards Stretford, Altrincham and the Mersey Valley along the towpath of the Bridgewater Canal, or into Tameside and the South Pennines alongside the recently restored and improved Ashton Canal. It is also possible to follow the Irwell Valley Way along the River Irwell from Salford Quays to Bury and Rossendale, a 30 miles walking route offering an astonishing mixture or urban and urban/rural fringe walking rich in industrial history as well as wildlife. Birmingham's canals also offer a superb choice of walking routes out into leafy Warwickshire. Edinburgh has a fascinating urban walkway along the banks of the stream known as the Water of Leith from Haymarket, in the city centre, to Leith Docks on the Firth of Forth, whilst Newcastle has its foot and cycle ways along the Tyne.

Cardiff has the 55 mile Taff Trail starting from the castle and its park in the centre of the city, following the River Taff via Llandaff and Pontypridd to Merthyr Tydfil, through a fascinating mixture of riverside, industrial and rural landscapes, past cathedrals, castles and reservoirs, eventually to reach Brecon Beacons National Park and Brecon town.

In these and many other industrial towns and cities, it is possible to devise a choice of walking routes through the city centres using a combination of still existing Victorian urban paths and alleyways between houses known in various parts of England as "ginnels", "twitchells" or "snickets". Unlike modern developers the Victorians retained ancient rural footpaths as useful pedestrian routes to shops and public transport. By linking such old ways, most now recorded on modern maps, through parks, allotment gardens, playing fields, cemeteries, and quieter streets, safe and pleasant through routes across parts of many Victorian cities can still be enjoyed.

Both Leeds and Sheffield cities are also fortunate enough to be served by the Trans Pennine Trail. This is a remarkable 350 miles (560km) traffic-free walking, cycling and horse-riding network of routes across the Pennines between Hornsea on the East Coast of England and Southport on the West Coast, with a key north-south axis between Leeds, Sheffield and Chesterfield, plus a spur from Selby to York. The Hull to Liverpool portion forms part of the 4,700 km E8, a massive European Long Distance Trail (assisted by ferries) extending from Cork in Southern Ireland to Istanbul, Turkey.

The Trans Pennine Trail uses, in the main, a combination of former railway track beds, canal towpaths, and sections of raised river embankment or levees. Much of the route is essentially urban walking and, because it penetrates city centres, it offers an opportunity to walk into and out of cities on entirely traffic free corridors. It is for its value for short suburb to city centre walking and cycling rather than long distance walking that the Trans-Pennine Trail will be most heavily used and valued.

The Leeds spur of the Trans Pennine Trail enters central Leeds along the towpath of the Aire and Calder Navigation and terminates at the canal basin of the Leeds & Liverpool canal. This 18th century canal towpath offers another superb green corridor for walkers and cyclists out of the city, through surprisingly unspoiled countryside, heading due westwards through the Aire Valley to the Yorkshire Dales and eventually to central Lancashire and finally to Liverpool.

It is not too fanciful in the case of Leeds, Manchester and Sheffield, or indeed for many other cities of a similar and smaller size such as York, Bradford, Edinburgh, Bristol, Bath, Exeter, Birmingham (with its superb canal towpath network), Manchester, Liverpool, Hull, Glasgow, Nottingham, Plymouth, Norwich and Ipswich, to envisage a network of utilitarian and leisure walking and cycling routes leading from the suburbs into the city centre. Such routes can and should be developed and promoted as city commuter routes. Even if they are used only one way, for example for a three or four mile brisk morning walk or jog into the office, returning by bus or train, this would have huge personal health benefits for commuters themselves and wider environmental benefits in terms of reduced congestion and pollution. Conversely such walking (and cycling) routes offer access into the wider countryside, using the precious green corridors formed by canal towpaths, riversides, or old railway line trackbeds such as the Sustrans Bristol-Bath Path.

Passageway or "ginnel" between 1970s' housing development. By retaining the right of way behind gardens, local communities enjoy quick and easy access on foot to nearby open countryside. Current trends are to close many such urban paths, allegedly to deter burglars or drug users, but this only increases car dependency.

London has of course long been a favourite place for urban leisure walkers from the time of Samuel Johnson onwards, and has the advantage of not only its rich heritage of open spaces but more recently the formally designated Thames Path National Trail. Another opportunity is the Lea Valley Walk, a 50 mile trail from the Limehouse Basin in East London through the Lea Valley (it may have to be diverted around the Olympic Village) to Luton, creating a north-south axis with the Thames Path. There are also several fine other cross-city strategic walking routes devised by Ramblers' Groups and individual London Boroughs including the exotically named Capital Ring, Jubilee Walkway, Jubilee Greenway, Green Chain Walk and London Loop.

London also enjoys one of the world's best public transport networks – bus, underground and suburban rail – so that it is possible to feed into London's footpath network at a variety of key points. Such core routes can have feeders from the suburbs utilising wherever possible traffic- calmed streets and Home Zones, surviving footpaths or bridleways, as well as protected green spaces.

Urban walking is an increasingly popular mode of more gentle walking. The Ramblers' in-house magazine, *Walk*, regularly features recommended urban walks in its pages, including heritage walks in and around towns and cities, together with the more usual out-of-town and deep countryside walks. The Association and its magazine fully recognise the importance of urban walking as a key leisure activity.

There is however a threat to the future of some, potentially important, urban paths. Recent changes to the Highways Act 1980 allow local authorities, on the advice of the police, to close sections of highways and paths – mainly urban alleyways – in areas of towns and cities affected by "high levels of crime". It is mainly aimed at areas where burglars are allegedly using public paths behind properties to access homes or drug dealing is prevalent. A further area of concern are paths through school playing fields, when it is felt, in some circles, that paedophiles could use a public path to access school premises or behave as voyeurs.

Above: Barges alongside busy warehouses at the canal basin in the centre of Leeds, about 1900. There is no possibility of canalside walking.

Below: Total transformation at the same location. Today the warehouses have given way to smart retail and office development – and it is possible to walk along both sides of the canal. (Yorkshire Post Newspapers)

The only real solution to the possible misuse of these new provisions is undoubtedly to ensure that many more walkers use such paths, which itself will help reduce anti-social activity.

What is also needed are robust Walking Strategies for every town and city in Britain, which will identify the network of key walking routes that can and should be promoted for both utilitarian and leisure use. Where necessary, new routes should be created to eliminate the need to walk along heavily trafficked roads. This can be achieved through the powers available to local authorities through existing highway legislation and through Rights of Way Improvement Plans. Such routes can provide valuable links with core routes into the town centre or local shopping and service centres and with public transport nodes. Greater public use and therefore vigilance of such routes will help reduce misuse by criminals and perverts. In any case children are at far, far greater risk from motor traffic, including parents driving their offspring to school in poor visibility 4x4s which are parked at or near school gates.

But perhaps the most positive development of all and antidote to path neglect and closure in smaller towns and larger villages is the Ramblers inspired Walkers are Welcome programme.

At the time of writing (2011) more than 52 small towns in England, Scotland and Wales have joined this initiative which began in Hebden Bridge in the South Pennines, but has spread throughout the UK. This is a community-led initiative in which enough local residents and the local authorities have to demonstrate their willingness to support the project before it can begin. The prime aim is to make the town centre and also its immediate locality a place where walkers are welcomed by guest houses, inns and specialist outdoor shops that meet walkers' needs. In addition, local walks from the town centres out into the surrounding countryside, all accessible by public transport, are developed and promoted through leaflets and websites. The distinctive Walkers are Welcome boot print logo appears in local shops and suppliers, and signifies a friendly and helpful welcome for people who arrive on foot.

But it also requires local communities and their elected representatives – Parish Councils and local authorities – to ensure that the local footpath network is put into first class order, that routes are properly signed and waymarked, that obstructions are removed. Volunteers from local Walkers are Welcome Committees and kindred groups assist with such efforts. This includes creating more and better walkways both within the town itself and leading from the town centres out into the nearby countryside. Urban paths are therefore especially valuable as ways of enjoying the town in question – a key aim – but are also a means to get out into the hinterland, on foot rather than by car, in some cases using linear routes which can be accessed by the local public transport network.

Sustainability and active travel are therefore at the heart of the Walkers are Welcome concept. It is about changing attitudes to local walking and its provision, getting people out of their cars and on to their feet, ensuring that expectations are met. It has an implicit message that you don't need a perhaps lengthy car journey to a distant National Park to enjoy a walk, which can literally be done from your own doorstep. The Walkers are Welcome campaign is aimed as much at local communities themselves as at their visitors.

These are yet early days, and it is too soon to assess the success or otherwise of the Walkers are Welcome movement. In each of the participating towns, there have been some excellent local walk publications produced. Some splendid work has been done in partnership with local authorities and local landowners to improve footpaths and make them more walker-friendly. Awareness of the many opportunities of local walks within and from each town centre has been raised. The omens are good.

7. WALKING FOR HEALTH

If medication existed which had a similar effect, it would be regarded as a 'wonder drug' or a 'miracle cure' – Liam Donaldson, former Government Chief Medical Officer

There is nothing new about recognising the value of walking to improve physical and mental health.

As long ago as 1913 that great founding father of the outdoor movement G.M.Trevelyan could write, in his celebrated essay on Walking:

I have two doctors, my left leg and my right. When body and mind are out of gear (and those twin parts of me live at such close quarters that one always catches melancholy from the other) I know that I have only to call in my doctors and I shall be well again.

Even in 1913 this was hardly a new thought. From the early 19th century onwards German, Austrian, Czech and Swiss spa towns had been offering carefully engineered panoramic hillside walking trails in the pure air of the nearby woods and mountain sides for their anaemic, tubercular and geriatric patients to tempt them out for a restorative walk between bouts of water-treatment. The concept of a "luft kurort", or spa town famed as much for the recuperative power of its good, clean air as for its mineral springs, still has a strong resonance in mainland Europe.

The fashion soon spread to England, with the building of German or Swiss style Kurhalle or Spa Pavilions for post-treatment concerts in towns such as Bath, Buxton, Cheltenham or Harrogate. Public gardens were laid out to encourage patients to take advantage of the clean air and exercise. Ilkley, a small former spa town in West Yorkshire on the edge of the Yorkshire Dales, attracted no less a figure than Charles Darwin to recuperate after completing his *The Origin of Species* in 1859. Ilkley has long lost its spa treatment establishments, but the well engineered "health" paths survive across nearby Ilkley Moor, complete with semi-artificial tarns and ornamental walkways, and carefully through local woods and by waterfalls such as in Heber's Ghyll. Latter day health seekers still enjoy the recuperative power of country walks along these mid Victorian trails.

There is ample scientific evidence to support the belief in the health value of walking activity, and to explain in particular why walking through areas of countryside and natural beauty is so important for restoring and maintaining physical and mental health.

The human body has evolved over millions of years in truly remarkable ways to allow us to walk upright, and to carry the weight of our relatively heavy heads and large brains above our frames. The structure of our skeletons and muscles has been described as a triumph of biological and mechanical engineering, allowing us to walk and run with ease.

Humans are literally built for walking. We may not be able to move across a flat plain anything like as fast as the larger quadrupeds, but what we lack in speed we make up for in agility. We can walk across rough, even rugged and steep terrain without difficulty. We are nimble and agile enough to go through forest, climb mountain sides, cross tundra or desert. We can cross rivers, climb ravines, and walk for many hours at a stretch.

Even in the relatively easy environments of a settled countryside, as any experienced walker will tell you, a country walk using a variety of different graded and surfaced footpaths and tracks across country is far less tiring than road-walking, using as you do different muscles for different slopes or surfaces. You are far less likely to get blisters on your heels in such territory than repetitively hammering along the hard, smooth surface of a long tarmac road, even though you can cover far more distance in an hour or a day along such a

Landscaped walkways were laid out around the Victorian spa town of Ilkley to encourage convalescing patients to complete their cure by taking healthy walks. Visitors could also take advantage of the town's clean air, which contrasted with the heavily smoke-polluted industrial cities of that era. (Dorian Speakman)

route.

Standing and sitting actually suits our bodies less well than walking. Standing still is actually quite hard for us to do – we must normally fidget and constantly move our weight around onto each foot and different muscles for comfort. Sitting, which most urban western people now do for many hours during even an average working day, can put pressure on our spine and cause tension in neck and back muscles, leading to headaches and back pain, sometimes with serious long-term consequences if posture is poor. When walking, we are paradoxically at our most relaxed, muscles are in balance, we breathe more easily, the natural swing of the arms balancing the motion of the legs.

It's only when our leg muscles are out of balance for whatever reason, such as bone, joint or muscular injury, that we realise how important this balance is when walking. Try walking more than a few metres, with different shoes with either a higher or lower heel, or wearing only one shoe, and the task soon becomes slow and painful.

The constant movement of muscles when walking, the increased circulation of the blood and expansion of the lungs, means that the whole body is invigorated. The very rhythm of walking, when you achieve a regular length of stride reflecting your height and leg length, determines your natural speed. This allows you to move almost unconsciously along, as the rhythm of the walk takes over. You can of course walk or run at a faster or stroll at a slower speed, perhaps reflecting the nature and gradient of the terrain, the urgency of the journey or the company you are with, but this ultimately requires more physical effort. At your natural speed walking becomes an unconscious process, allowing you to relax, think, take in your surroundings, talk to a companion, even if it happens to be of the canine variety. Hence its huge therapeutic powers.

Above all, walking in a relaxed way, is a highly pleasurable activity.

But one reason why many people, even some at relatively youthful ages, are no longer able or feel able to walk is obesity. If you are overweight, walking even a short distance on level ground becomes an enormous effort. So you walk even less, weight increases, muscles deteriorate and the vicious spiral continues.

This is now so prevalent a situation in contemporary Britain and the USA in particular (though other western countries are rapidly catching up) that it constitutes perhaps the greatest single threat to human health and well being – a potential social and economic catastrophe as health

services can no longer cope with the consequent rising costs of dealing with the escalating problem.

So how did this situation come about?

The human species evolved as hunters and gatherers, and later as farmers, through millennia when food was scarce and could only be achieved by considerable physical effort, whether hunting, herding or ploughing. Even in the industrial revolution, heavy manual labour – in the construction industries, in mines, steel works, docks, railways, mills and in domestic service – use of human muscle power in manufacturing and services industries was the norm. Most people also walked to work – though mills and factories were usually much closer to home.

Only in the last half century or so has this radically changed. Most manual jobs have largely been replaced by automation and electronic or mechanical processes, requiring tasks during the undertaking of which we spend most of our time sitting.

Walking is a simple form of health-giving exercise that can benefit all ages. Here a family enjoys a section of The Ridgeway National Trail near Wendover, Buckinghamshire. (Natural England – Jos Joslin)

Depending too much on the convenience of the car for all leisure travel needs can lead to lack of physical exercise and future health problems related to obesity.

Even a generation ago, people were more physically active – they walked more, used public transport (which required walking to and from the bus or tram stop or railway station) and had physically demanding jobs in factories, mills or mines which required high outputs of physical energy. Less sophisticated domestic appliances required harder physical work in the home. Now jobs are mainly office based, less physically demanding, and require the worker to sit in front of a computer screen or at a telephone desk for most of the day.

Children also lead far less physically active lives. They are no longer allowed or encouraged to play in the street or the local park because of the perceived danger from traffic or paedophiles, and spend many more hours sitting in front of a television screen or games console. School sports and outdoor activities have been reduced because of the selling off of playing fields and ever narrower national curricula. It has been suggested that the present generation of children are so physically unfit and overweight they could be the first generation in UK history to be frequently outlived by their parents.

Most journeys by adults and children in Britain are now undertaken in the comfort and warmth of a private car, without even the need to walk to a bus stop.

Yet our intake of food and the nature of our high calorie diet still reflects the more physically active lifestyles of our ancestors. The result is that many of us have put on what in the eyes of most doctors are alarming amounts of additional body weight.

Obesity is now regarded by health professionals as one of the greatest threats to human health in the western world. At present 9,000 adults in the UK die a premature death each year due to obesity-related illness. It is estimated that physical inactivity is now costing the National Health Service £9.2 billion per annum. Bizarrely this also includes the need to build larger hospital beds, seats, patient facilities and even coffins for people who are grossly overweight.

But there is also a terrible personal cost. Being obese puts you at greater risk of getting high blood pressure, Type 2 diabetes, heart disease, osteoarthritis, strokes, and many forms of cancer. All these conditions are more prevalent and harder to deal with among people who are seriously overweight.

The growth in obesity among the adult population in the UK is alarming. In 1980 just 6% of adults were classified as clinically obese. By 2004 this had shot up to a terrifying 24% – a 400% increase. This percentage continues to grow, with a third of all adults predicted to be obese by 2012. You only have to look in any shopping mall or any public space to notice the high percentage of relatively young adults with bulging midriffs who find walking and sometimes even balance difficult because of their size.

It is not just adults but many children who are now judged to be chronically obese, whose lives are likely to be shortened as a result of the damage caused to their bodily function and immune systems.

Obesity does not happen overnight – most weight gain takes place over many years and can result from an average daily energy imbalance (calorie intake being higher than calorie output) of just 1% to 2% per day over a long period.

Perhaps the single most potent source of obesity is car dependency. The evidence of the serious damage to health caused by car-dominated lifestyles is overwhelming. Dr Adrian Davis, a leading UK expert on the impacts of transport on health, has pointed out the exact parallels between rising car ownership and usage in the UK and obesity. Not only do numbers of cars per head of population reflect obesity levels, but the private car-based land-use development patterns and the investment in roads also profoundly affect physical activity levels. Davis points to research in the USA, Australia and China where there is a significant association between commuting to work by car and obesity compared with the more physically active travel modes – walking and cycling – together with public transport use. He also points to research that suggests a significant co-relation between car use and physical inactivity – the more you drive, the less you walk and cycle. Each additional hour spent in a car results in a 6% greater likelihood of obesity, but every additional kilometre walked per day is linked to a 4.8% reduction in obesity.

Most startling of all perhaps is the well-documented study in China of adult males who acquired their first car between 1989 and 1997. On average Chinese men studied gained 1.8kg within a year of acquiring their vehicle and consequently had a 70% greater chance of becoming obese. But this is not just a Chinese phenomenon. People living in car-free households in the UK walk about 131 more miles per year than the main driver in a car owning household; Davis estimates this could make an individual weight difference over a decade of up to 14 kilogrammes or 2 stones.

Even though 25% of all car journeys are less than two miles in length, and many could easily be replaced by walking (which in urban traffic conditions is actually almost as quick), it isn't just a question of human laziness. We are now in a situation when driving or being driven rather than walking even extremely short distances has become normal, accepted behaviour for children as well as adults.

The decline of walking is not just a result of the growth in the ownership and use of the car. It is the result of a dominant car culture which, as we have seen in early chapters, has transformed our lives to make ownership of a car, for most people, to be perceived as essential and the socially acceptable norm if they wish to access many facilities and services even when alternatives are actually available. By promoting their facilities almost exclusively for the motorised customer or visitor, many service providers – including managers of countryside tourist attractions – constantly reinforce the belief that if you can't drive there you can't get there.

Dr Mayer Hillman, the lifelong campaigner for greener transport, also puts the blame firmly on successive generations of policy makers who have failed to recognise the importance of walking as an efficient as well as a healthy means of travel. Over the last 30 years, in both urban and rural areas, he notes that both new urban and new rural development have increasingly favoured or even determined the use of the private car as the prime means of access to services and facilities This in return deters people from cycling and walking:

the dangers posed by increased car use make it less safe and therefore less likely that other people will make their journeys by cycle or on foot. Survey after survey in the high-car ownership world reveals that the majority of the population – young and old alike – are getting insufficient exercise and are therefore at greater risk of heart disease and other life-threatening and debilitating illnesses. They are also denied the enhancement that improved fitness brings to the quality of their lives and to their mental well-being.

Recent research by the World Cancer Research Fund estimated that over 10,000 cases of breast and bowel cancer could be prevented each year if people did more brisk walking and other forms of regular activity. In 2010, the Fund launched its Walking Together campaign to raise awareness of the role walking can have in cancer prevention.

But walking is a human activity which provides more than just physical benefit to the walker. Recent research has shown that people, irrespective of income, who have access to green open spaces, to woods, parks, fields and footpaths, enjoy better mental as well as physical health and a better quality of life than those who only have access to a predominantly urban environment.

Dr William Bird, a General Practitioner, established the first Health Walk scheme in South Oxfordshire in 1995 to help maintain levels of physical activity in a particular local community. The walks were designed to increase fitness and improve health, but crucially, the main motivation for people to come out on the walks was to access the local countryside.

Bird was among the first formally to recognise the value to health professionals of what has been dubbed the "Green Gym" of the great outdoors in

Walking for Health encourages more people to become active in their communities – this group in Grimsby are starting their walk from the town's busy suburbs. (Natural England / Walking for Health – Paul Glendell)

A Walking for Health group enjoying a bluebell wood in Roosthole, West Sussex. (Natural England / Walking for Health – Paul Glendell)

dealing not only with the physical problems of obesity, but also mental problems – depression, anxiety and other forms of mental illness and disability:

The countryside can be seen as a great outpatient department whose therapeutic value is yet to be fully realised. Research on two national schemes shows people are more likely to continue physical activity if this includes close contact with nature. Therefore harnessing a rise in leisure walking within green space could offer an unlimited resource to increase levels of physical activity in the UK.

By 2004 there were over 350 similar schemes to the Health Walk programme, by now co-ordinated by the British Heart Foundation and the Countryside Agency in their Walking the Way to Health Initiative. It was recognised that even just 30 minutes' brisk walk per day can achieve at least the minimum requirements to maintain good health and increasing this can improve overall standards of fitness. But many patients literally have to be taught how to walk. Starting off from easy strolls of just ten minutes, to eventually 30 minutes and eventually to walks of two or three miles, patients can build up their strength and self reliance to gradually enjoy greater degrees of mobility and personal freedom.

Walking for Health (WfH), as the Initiative is now known in England, has grown to become a major national programme of activity co-ordinated by Natural England (as successor to the Countryside Agency) to encourage people to get out into their local countryside on foot. There is an emphasis on using paths and open spaces close to or within towns – urban walking – rather than requiring a drive or public transport trip to areas further afield. This enables and encourages people to use their local countryside for repeat and independent activity.

By 2011 there were over 600 local WfH individual projects in England, with over 3,800 trained walk leaders available to take groups out, and 66,000 people taking part in local walks every week into

their local countryside. This has extended to encouraging access to open spaces further afield as part of what is now dubbed The Natural Health Service, recognising the powerful support leisure walking in natural surroundings can give to illness prevention as well as to patients in recovery from a variety of mental and physical conditions.

Medical science suggests that walking in great open spaces, such as within a National Park, is of enormous value to mental as well as physical health and well being – the finest form of preventive medicine. Shafts of sunlight are on the Hole of Horcum, as two walkers stride through this splendid part of the North York Moors National Park. (Yorkshire Post Newspapers)

Helen Phillips, Chief Executive Officer of Natural England, reports that every £1 invested by the Department of Health in WfH projects saves the National Health Service £7.18 in patient care costs – a sevenfold payback in investment, and huge endorsement of walking as a preventive medicine.

Walking for Health walks are very much aimed at giving people confidence in their own ability to use their own muscle power even for a relatively short and level walk, but there is also the social benefit of meeting other people and the security of being in a group. Because walking facilitates social contact for people who otherwise would be isolated, specialist groups have been devised – including women's groups and ethnic minorities – to help develop new supportive social networks. There is an official accreditation scheme so that Walking for Health groups can become recognised, using the national logo, provided they meet certain agreed standards and criteria. Primary Care Trusts are now heavily involved in Walking for Health and can direct patients to such groups. It is now possible for GPs to "prescribe" a programme of walks with a local group as a part of a patient's recovery programme and as a preventive medicine.

Scotland has similar, very successful schemes, known as Paths to Health when established in 2001 and now known as Paths for All. This is a national charity, supported by Scottish Natural Heritage, the Scottish Government and NHS Health Scotland as well as ScotRail and the Centre for Healthy Working Lives.

In Wales, Let's Walk Cymru established by the Countryside Council for Wales, and now supported by Sport Council Wales and Health Challenge of Wales, has taken on the co-ordinating role for a flourishing programme of Walking for Health groups. Let's Walk Cymru is about building on the Walking for Health initiative, promoting walks to include a variety of organisations' guided and self-guided walk programmes, including Nordic Walking and cross-country orienteering to encourage participants to take part in more ambitious walking activity in the Welsh countryside.

These are, of course, variously enhanced forms of healthy walk activity, which have their own followers both in the UK and overseas. Nordic Walking, that is walking using two walking poles, originated from Ski Walking, an out-of-season walking activity in skiing resorts in Scandinavia using ski sticks. Use of the twin lightweight poles increases arm and upper body exercise activity, burns more calories but is also judged to reduce pressure on hip, knees and ankle joints as well as assisting balance and hill climbing activity. Techniques have to be practised, but Nordic Walking is claimed to offer better overall exercise benefits.

There are also more commercial organisations now offering help and advice on various fitness regimes and walking techniques such as Joanna Hall's Walk Active Club. It offers a range of much more energetic activities, with a UK-wide programme of walks, courses and trainers linked to literature and a range of promotional goods designed to encourage people to improve their fitness primarily by walking.

Such more sophisticated developments to the Walking the Way to Health concept are clearly welcome, but walking remains a simple, easily accessible activity for all and requires the minimum amount of skill or equipment to participate. Encouraging leisure walking is therefore a prime, low cost method of combating the many health problems caused by obesity.

But as William Bird and others have shown, such programmes need to be intimately linked with the safeguarding of public footpaths and open spaces, and ensuring ease of safe access to them in both town and countryside.

Work by Dr Richard Mitchell of the University of Glasgow has explored how access to "green space" can be of special value to people from poorer backgrounds in terms of health benefits. Access to parks, playing fields, local woods, can bring real benefits to the whole community. By examining mortality rates for over 366,000 individuals between 2001 and 2005, Mitchell noted that whilst there was a notable gap between the mortality rates of rich and poorer people, the gap was much narrower in areas where poorer people have good access to green space.

In other words there is measurable, significant health benefit and therefore economic benefit in giving everyone access to the countryside. A green and accessible environment promotes good health and helps to save medical and social care and other costs. This is true not only for countryside close to towns and cities but also for Britain's great protected landscapes – the National Parks, Heritage Coasts and Areas of Outstanding Natural Beauty – that should be equally accessible for green walks to the whole population, not just to the more mobile and affluent, in order to secure long-term health benefits for the UK population as a whole.

Carl Lis, the chairman of the United Kingdom Association of National Park Authorities, has suggested that active enjoyment of National Parks should have a key role in both physical and mental health improvement, and on the difficult to define concept of well-being. "What value can you place on the smiling faces on those walkers out there?" he argues. "What could be better for health and well-being than enjoying the peace and tranquillity of the Three Peaks or going out in the Lakes or the North York Moors? I'd love to see the benefits of these places recognised in terms of the country's agenda."

In 2010 the National Trust also launched a major new initiative Outdoor Nation which aims to encourage the British public to make more use of the Trust's gardens, parks, hills and coastlines for walking and outdoor activity. The aim is to enable more people, especially over-protected city-dwelling children, addicted to television and computer screens, who are "terrified" of the unknown countryside, to reconnect with the natural world by spending more time walking in Britain's magnificent green spaces. Dame Fiona Reynolds, Director-General of the National Trust, herself a "passionate walker", emphasises the mental and psychological benefits a country walk can bring: "When you are walking everything calms down, you can think clearly, you can breathe fresher air. It can be a form of preventive medicine. Walking is a brilliant way to find yourself, to give yourself space."

But important as the Walks for Health programme and the Outdoor Nation campaign are, they will not succeed unless they result in a fundamental change of lifestyle for the majority of their participants, away from sedentary towards a more active way of life.

This isn't just a matter of walking more – there are lots of other excellent indoor and outdoor physical activities which can help to increase fitness and reduce the risk of obesity. Swimming and cycling, jogging, climbing, canoeing and tennis can all, if combined with a balanced diet, achieve major weight reduction and health benefits.

Walking has the key advantage compared with most other physical and sporting activities in that it requires no specialist equipment – a pair of sturdy trainers and a waterproof jacket is adequate for most situations – nor is there any cost, payment or pre-planning required to take part, apart from perhaps a bus fare or a modest amount of petrol if the walk isn't to start from home. And it's equally available to people of all ages, genders, physical abilities and diverse ethnic backgrounds.

There is something innately ridiculous about driving some distance to a gym to spend an hour on a powered walking treadmill or stationary cycle, staring at a television screen or listening to an MP3, when a brisk walk or cycle ride through local countryside could have achieved the same benefits in a health-giving greener environment at a fraction of the cost.

The other huge advantage of walking against most formal team and competitive sports is that it doesn't require intensive training to enjoy or to remain "competitive". It is also something you can continue to do throughout your life, especially as there is far less risk of injury than in the popular physical contact sports. Not many people continue to play soccer or tennis into their eighties, but lots of walkers most certainly do continue to walk at such ages. It is an activity that does so much to prolong their active lives.

Medical opinion agrees that even just half an hour's moderate exercise a day can make a real difference to maintaining overall physical health, quality of life and well being. A reasonably brisk walk, every day, of just a couple of miles, preferably with at least some gradient along the route, can make a big difference to how the body copes with sedentary living.

Ultimately it is about a lifestyle change. To achieve long lasting physical and psychological benefit from walking you need to build it into every aspect of life. You need to reduce the amount of time spent sitting indoors or in a car, to replace at least some car and even bus journeys by walking or cycling, to make walking, for both leisure and utilitarian purposes, a central part of living.

But for many people, such a change in lifestyle could represent a considerable challenge.

8. WALKING FOR THE EARTH – LIVING A CAR-FREE LIFESTYLE

I believe that we are witnessing an historical moment when the huge danger to the environment is so evident that we must conceive a new responsibility with respect to the future – César Manrique 1992

Walking as an activity, in the UK at least, faces an acute paradox.

As a mode of travel it is in decline – though this may soon change. But as a leisure activity it is in significant growth. The Ramblers' Association claim, with justification, that walking is Britain's most popular outdoor leisure activity. Surveys suggest that 77% of UK adults walk for pleasure at least once a month. 44.5% claim to go for a walk over two miles at least once every four weeks. Over seven million people walk in the countryside every week, emphasising the importance of walking as a core, sustainable tourist activity. Membership of the Ramblers' Association – now known simply as The Ramblers – has more than more than tripled since the 1980s to over 123,000.

At the heart of this paradox is the attitude we have to our cars. To suggest that British people have a love affair with their cars is an understatement. For the vast majority of car owners, the car is choice, the car is freedom. The car provides access to a huge range of facilities and services, and is an enabler for a huge range of lifestyle choices. Journeys which would otherwise take hours on foot or by public transport (where it exists), or simply not be possible, can take mere minutes. A car is also a mobile holdall, able to carry everything you need for a day out in the country, food, water, even a change of clothes. This is especially valuable if you have younger children who need a buggy or carrier and changing facilities. It is also an essential requirement if you have a disability, a mobility impairment, or have an elderly or disabled relative.

We have lived through decades since World War II during which car ownership and usage have become increasingly affordable to ordinary people. Never since its invention have cars been cheaper to purchase nor petrol (in real terms) less expensive. Mass car ownership has offered the majority of people lifestyle opportunities that previous generations could only dream of.

And nothing has encouraged leisure walking in the countryside more effectively than rising car ownership and improvements to the road network to give access to that countryside. Huge investment in the motorway and trunk road network over the last 50 years now allows city dwellers to reach our National Parks and Areas of Outstanding Natural Beauty, Heritage Coasts or National Trust estates from almost anywhere in the UK in a matter of hours. Constant investment in car-related infrastructure such as car parks, access roads and visitor centres close to car parks has reinforced this ease of access. A process that began when the first railway lines were built into the countryside, and increased in the pre- and post war periods with the growth of motor bus networks, has now become an avalanche on rubber tyres.

Over 90% of visitors to our National Parks now arrive by car, leaving less than 10% for all other modes of travel – coaches and minibuses, cycling, walking and public transport which in most National Parks accounts for no more than around 3% of visitors. This is equally true of Areas of Outstanding Natural Beauty, Heritage Coasts, Country Parks and National Trust properties. Only urban parks and some areas of countryside close to towns have a higher percentage of non-car visitors and they are mainly dog walkers who live in the immediate locality and are exercising their pets from home.

But the car has also changed the nature of leisure

walking. Guidebooks to countryside walks are now almost all exclusively aimed at car users, and focus on short circular walks from and to the car park. The trend over recent years has been for ever-shorter walks. Few authors even bother to mention the existence of local bus or train services, even if the walk starts at or close to a bus stop or a railway station. Linear or point-to-point walks that are dependent on public transport have little appeal to publishers or to guidebook readers. Only long distance walks are less reliant on car access, but even then people will go to enormous lengths to use two cars and two drivers or be collected by a relative or friend in a car rather than suffer the indignity of having to use a bus or train to return from the end of a Long Distance Trail.

Walkers waiting for the returning Settle-Carlisle train to Leeds at Ribblehead in the heart of the Yorkshire Dales National Park. Threatened with closure in the 1980s, this is now one of the most popular local train services in England for walkers, with regular guided walks from local stations arranged every weekend.

Programmes of guided walks provided by local authorities and even voluntary bodies such as The Ramblers almost invariably start from a car park. These walks are often in locations and at times which make it impossible for non car owners to take part (typically leaving ten minutes before the arrival of a bus), though there are notable exceptions, such as RA Groups and Areas both in London and in some northern cities who still offer public transport based walks, as well as committed "green travel" groups such as the Dales Rail and Wales Rail Ramblers, and the DalesBus Ramblers. Walking clubs will often give a grid location as an instruction to park in a remote location (leaving their vehicles as clear targets for car thieves) or, if they actually have some concerns about reducing the number of cars littering the countryside, will meet at a car-accessible out of town location even to car share.

Little wonder public transport users feel marginalised. While costs of car travel have declined in real terms, public transport costs – both rail and bus – have accelerated faster than inflation. Only the introduction of free Concessionary Pass travel for the over-sixties on local bus networks has, in recent years, helped to reverse this trend, but how long this facility will continue is difficult to judge.

In so many respects fast, easy and inexpensive access to the countryside is a phenomenon to celebrate. Car ownership has arguably been as important as countryside legislation in creating magnificent new access opportunities to the countryside for millions of people who would not otherwise be able to get there. Access to a car for a trip to the countryside is especially valued to those very many people who have mobility problems, whether it is caused by old age, infirmity, a debilitating illness or condition. The car is of especial value to families, enabling groups of different ages and physical ability to travel together in speed and comfort. No one would wish to reverse this.

For most people owning a car – which has high fixed costs in terms of its purchase, tax, insurance and maintenance, but low marginal costs of usage – is a liberating experience. The alternative of using public transport is not a realistic choice. It might require perhaps half a mile walk to the nearest bus stop, waiting for a bus which may or may not turn up (and may not run at all on a Sunday, the most popular day for leisure travel), paying perhaps several pounds in fares for two or three people for a short journey. You are also limited to undertake a walk when you arrive at your destination that starts close to the bus route and can be completed in time for a convenient return bus.

You might however be prepared to park at a railway station and take a train because of the advantage a train has in speed and freedom from the problems of congestion, plus the ability a train offers to complete station-to-station linear walks. Scenic railways such as the Settle-Carlisle line through the Yorkshire Dales, the Hope Valley line through the Peak District, the Caldervale line in the South Pennines, the Esk Valley line through the North York Moors, the Conwy Valley line in Snowdonia and the scenic branch lines in Devon and Cornwall have been able to capture at least some walkers prepared to park, ride and walk.

Likewise some well marketed leisure bus networks in areas such as the Pembrokeshire Coast with its superb Puffin coastal bus network, the Norfolk Coast Hopper, the Shropshire Shuttle in the Shropshire Hills, the Roman Wall bus in Northumberland, Moorsbus in the North York Moors, the Dartmoor Sunday Rover network, the Stagecoach network in the Lake District and DalesBus in the Yorkshire Dales have all been able to appeal to at least some leisure walkers with cars. They are those prepared to park, ride and walk, and especially those doing linear walks. But even these highly attractive and well-promoted bus-and-walk trips to the countryside are used by a relatively small minority of potential users.

For most people the car is, and will remain, their first choice of accessing the countryside, and bus travel is generally seen to be a "distress purchase" – something to be used only when you have no other choice.

One huge additional benefit of the car revolution is that it has enabled rural tourism to grow and expand in areas well away from public transport hubs or corridors. No longer are visitors confined to rail or bus-served "resorts" but are able to visit – and walk – in once relatively remote rural areas well away from public transport. This has brought huge economic benefit to rural communities through rural tourism which is almost totally car-dependent.

For rural populations likewise car ownership has been a boon and helped to raise standards of living and quality of life in ways which would have been unimaginable in previous times.

All this is unarguable.

There is, however, a huge downside. Motor traffic is now a major threat to the environment. This includes C02 and other toxic emissions, including nitrogen oxides and particulates, especially from diesel engines.

But there are other major environmental impacts. Within our most precious protected landscapes, which by definition are protected because of their unspoiled beauty, there can be severe visual blight from traffic or parked cars at popular times. This impact is at its worst on fine summer weekends and at holiday periods with lines of vehicles being driven or parked along even minor roads, and severe traffic congestion at popular times in popular places and above all intrusive traffic noise which can destroy any sense of tranquillity. The very peace, quiet and unspoiled visual beauty that visitors seek and local communities deserve is threatened by their own actions in driving and parking their cars.

Visitor traffic also brings physical danger and threat to other road users. Heavy traffic is a major deterrent to walking and cycling especially on narrow country roads which have no side pavement. Wildlife is at risk. There is also significant disruption suffered by local communities in terms of congestion and parking problems, noise, and both visual and air pollution.

There is another related issue. Vehicles need roads. It has been calculated that every single car on the road requires approximately 25 square metres of land. This is not just the area covered by a typical vehicle parked in a garage or parking bay, but the parking space required at the destination – the large concrete or tarmac car park to serve the office or shopping mall that has to be provided. In addition is the space needed on all our public roads to allow every new vehicle that is purchased to be driven. Lack of road space is a prime cause of congestion, but there is simply not enough land available in our towns and cities to cater for current levels of unrestricted demand.

If this seems an exaggeration, reflect on the huge space in towns and city centres now sterilised for car parking, and even in the countryside at any visitor attraction. The amount of garden space converted to concrete in millions of suburban homes to create a parking lot is, it is believed, a major contributor to urban flooding as rain water loses huge areas of natural soil drainage to car parks. The concrete required for road building and parking areas also has to be quarried. Quarries are a major blight in many of our finest upland limestone landscapes, including the Peak District, the Yorkshire Dales and the Mendips. Road improvement schemes, including new bypasses and even motorways within protected landscapes to carry traffic from their urban catchment towns, also blight and compromise landscape quality.

Cars also require significant material and energy requirements for their construction and scrapping, all of which have emission implications. This is equally true of other forms of mechanised transport – trains, buses and even cycles. However a typical diesel or electric train has a life expectancy of around thirty years, a bus of around twenty years but a car a mere ten.

But cars like any other piece of modern technology are not the problem. It is the way cars are used that raises complex issues, as indeed Colin Buchanan forecast over forty years ago.

To understand these issues, it might be useful to consider how most car-users can be fitted into three broad categories, a spectrum which extends from the occasional, somewhat reluctant car user, to those for whom the car is an essential part of the process of living.

This has considerable implications for understanding who does and who does not walk and how walking can be encouraged, as the evidence is that the more you drive, the less you walk.

The Pembrokeshire coast boasts some of the UK's most dramatic coastal scenery. Walkers have easy access through the excellent Puffin bus network.

DalesBus Ramblers catching the return Sunday afternoon 874 bus from Kettlewell in Upper Wharfedale after a day's walk in the hills.

The Discretionary Users – around 10% of drivers.

Discretionary Users are people who have a car available either in their own garage, or perhaps are members of a car club. This is an increasingly attractive option for many Discretionary Users, who use the vehicle only when no other viable option is available. They will walk, cycle, use the bus or train for most daily journeys and only use the vehicle when it is absolutely necessary – at times when there is no public transport, to help someone with a disability, to carry heavy goods and shopping. These people - the reluctant drivers – are less dependent on a car and could most easily be persuaded to give up their vehicle, especially if the option of hiring a car or sharing a car club vehicle was readily available for those relatively few car-essential occasions. Discretionary Users are likely to walk and cycle much more than their more car-dependent neighbours.

The Car Reliant – about 30% of all drivers

Car reliant people are a far higher percentage of the population than discretionary car users. These are people whose lives and access to services and facilities would be significantly curtailed if a car was no longer available. They have taken decisions on where to live and how to travel to work or for leisure that assume the regular availability of at least one car in the household. They may also be regular users of public transport, for example to commute to work, especially if it can be shown that using a bus or train is cheaper and easier because of lack of or the cost of parking. But they may prefer to park at a railway station with its more reassuring structure of shelter, timetables and tracks to catch a train rather than walk to the nearest but more isolated and less reassuring bus stop.

Good quality public transport – which includes good quality information – and the creation of safe and pleasant walking and cycling routes in town and in countryside are in fact likely to persuade such people to use their cars less and walk and cycle more – with consequent benefits to their health and to the environment.

Discretionary Users and the Car Reliant should be the prime target for policy makers to achieve the much needed "modal shift" away from car usage towards the greener modes of travel.

The Car Dependent – about 60% of all drivers.

Sadly in contemporary Britain this includes the majority of the population for whom a car has become an essential part of their lives, and without which they would feel totally physically and psychologically stranded and helpless. They are most likely to live in two, three or even four car households. They will probably live in rural areas or outer suburbs and will rarely, if ever, use public transport apart from commuting from a railhead into a congested city centre or into London. But they will also include many poorer rural or semi-rural families, barely able to keep a single car on the road, for whom a car is their only mode of transport because they live in a rural area – the transport poor. It is interesting to note that the least affluent members of society, even when living in towns with good bus services, are often more likely to use taxis – car substitutes – than the local bus network, simply because they don't understand how public transport works in terms of routes, fares and the need to plan your journey in advance, all important life-skills.

To some extent the Car Dependent have already taken a lifestyle choice decision which has committed them, irrevocably, to the car. For example if you choose to live in an isolated farmhouse in Upper Teesdale or the middle of Dartmoor, then the logic is to acquire, or try to acquire, a car for every adult member of the household to give them independence. But even people living in far less isolated situations, such as on the edge of a small country town or outer city suburb, may adopt such a lifestyle from choice. It is, in the UK at least, "normal" behaviour.

This doesn't necessarily mean that such people are physically inactive. They may be frequent walkers, driving out to the nearest country park, National Trust property or even National Park, following the well used circular walks promoted in all the pamphlets. Their high degree of personal mobility will also give them access to many other outdoor activities – mountain biking (with bikes carried on the back or roof of the vehicle), swimming, playing tennis or golf.

But a high percentage of these Car Dependent people easily become almost totally physically inactive, so that the vehicle becomes a prop and a comfort zone – a motorised personal perambulator required for even the shortest journey. For the Car Dependent, buses are often a complete mystery, walking a strenuous and unpleasant activity exposed to dangers, strangers and the general discomfort of wind and rain. A car is simple to understand, will go anywhere exactly when you want, and is a home on wheels. This is where the risks of obesity become all too real, as sedentary lifestyles increasingly reduce the ability to walk all but the shortest distances.

If for any reason the car is off the road, the Car Dependent are lost. You hear stories of elderly people who, when they can no longer drive because of physical frailty, feel they have lost all independence, and rapidly give up the will to live. Walking or using a bus is an ordeal which physically or psychologically they simply cannot cope with any more.

This also explains the extreme vocal reaction which invariably accompanies any attempt to curb or limit the "freedom" of the driver to take his or her vehicle anywhere in most towns or in the countryside, and to park that car anywhere without charge or hindrance. These people fully sympathised with and even supported the petrol protesters, the truck drivers ready to protest at any attempt to tax or increase the costs of petrol or diesel at the pump. The Car Dependent firmly believe in the "right to drive". These were the people who, in 2000, inflicted the first and perhaps most grievous dent in the Blair Government's green agenda by forcing the abandonment of the "fuel duty escalator" whereby fuel tax was to rise faster than inflation to help woo the nation away from oil-dependency. Protests at the petrol pumps and power stations caused a Government U-turn, which has had severe and continuing consequences in terms of transport and energy efficiency agendas. Persuading such people to change their behaviour is extremely difficult unless they are forced to do so by disability or financial pressures.

*

These three categories are not static or mutually exclusive, but form part of an overall spectrum, or pyramid, with the Discretionary Users at the top of the pyramid, and the most Car Dependent – and numerous – at the bottom. You may, at various stages of your life, move between categories, which form part of a spectrum. You may start your adult life living in a city centre as a student, only acquiring a car in your first job that you use just at weekends. Marriage and a family make you more Car Reliant as the children arrive, but in middle years you may move into the country and live in a small village or isolated hamlet where parents and children in their late teens all have access to their own vehicle. In later years when driving and traffic becomes more of an ordeal you may begin to walk more and finally have to give up the car and move back into a town in your last years, once again depending, probably very reluctantly, on walking and lifts from friends for most journey needs.

Partly as a result of brilliant marketing, cars are not only one of the most important consumer items we possess, but are presented by manufacturers and advertisers as key lifestyle indicators, reflecting our status, personality and identity. Brand is important. Our status is defined by what we drive. For many people, especially younger and middle aged males, driving is a form of pleasurable activity that gives both freedom and exhilaration, especially when driving at speed, that few other activities match. They are in control. Any attempt to restrict, curb or even manage that freedom of choice provokes an irrational and angry response.

City centre parking controls and congestion however are seen as inevitable, and drivers, albeit reluctantly, are prepared to pay for scarce parking space – and maybe equally reluctantly, use alternative means such as public transport including park and ride systems for a commuter trip into town.

In rural areas, however, congestion is rarely perceived as a problem. Even conditions of fairly extreme rural congestion along narrow lanes, in areas such as the Lake District and Peak District, with traffic queues at every junction, are perceived as normal by urban drivers, despite the impact on the landscape and on other non-motorised road users.

It is noteworthy how many national and local amenity organisations, such as CPRE, the National Trust, the Ramblers' Association, Civic Trusts and Friends of the Lake District, have over the years led valiant campaigns for traffic management in National Parks and other areas of protected countryside. However their grass-root members have done the opposite, and have often been highly vocal in their opposition to any green transport or traffic management schemes. Despite the National Trust's strong green travel policies, a proposal by its Council in 2005 to charge members to park at its properties was heavily defeated at the AGM, with one of the biggest responses from the ordinary membership the Trust had ever seen.

With the notable exception of the Campaign for National Parks, which still sees traffic pollution as a major issue in UK National Parks, most national amenity bodies have quietly dropped any high profile support for traffic management in the countryside. Despite motor traffic having by far the greatest negative environmental impact of any visitor activity, this is now deemed by senior management to be a too politically sensitive issue to be tackled.

One reason for this apparent weakness in face of the car lobby is that National Park Authorities in the UK have also suffered a series of resounding defeats over the last few decades with even quite modest traffic management schemes, which have been defeated by vocal local opposition. Examples of traffic management or modest parking control schemes that have bitten the dust include Burrator on Dartmoor, Gordale in the Yorkshire Dales, along the Military Road Roman Wall in Northumberland, Blakey Ridge in the North York Moors. In Snowdonia the Green Keys project, designed to rationalise and charge for on-road parking, produced a backlash in the outdoor press which forced both the Ramblers and the British Mountaineering Association to backtrack on their initial support for the project. Even the Peak District National Park Authority with successful schemes in the Goyt and Derwent Valleys – both schemes that originated in the 1970s when opposition to traffic managed schemes was less organised and less vocal – were forced quietly to shelve the more radical version of the Derwent Valley Park-and-Ride scheme.

Drivers do it more carefully – a pioneering traffic management scheme in the New Forest introduced 40mph speed limits on the main A35 through the Forest. The object was to reduce deaths and injury to New Forest Ponies – as well as to humans.

Even the current fashion for Sustainable Visitor Travel Plans – aiming to promote walking, cycling and public transport usage to and within heritage sites, nature reserves and protected landscapes together with careful traffic management to reduce environmental impacts – suffers from a lack of political will and consequent funding priorities for their implementation. This ensures that little ever happens. Integrated Transport Strategies and Countryside Management Plans continue to play lip service to the concept of achieving modal shift in travel to and within the countryside. But actual, well-funded programmes of action to get people out of their cars and to walk, cycle or use shuttle bus services are notable by their absence.

So does this mean that the future of walking for all but a small minority of people in Britain – non car owners and a percentage of the Discretionary Users – is largely going to be as a leisure activity

Crowded car park at Capel Curig, Snowdonia. Around ninety per cent of all visitors to UK National Parks arrive by car, leading to traffic congestion and overflowing car parks at peak times.

A full car park with Bank Holiday traffic queuing to get in at Brimham Rocks, a popular Nidderdale visitor attraction in an Area of Outstanding Natural Beauty.

undertaken by car owners almost exclusively from a rural car park?

The most naive way of looking at the future is to assume that all present trends will continue. It is in fact very unlikely that cheap energy, and the near universal car ownership and unrestricted car usage of the present time will remain the norm in the decades ahead.

We may be already coming to the end of the age of car-based hyper-mobility. Even setting aside the likely catastrophic impacts of global warming on the UK and the world economy, it seems probable that we are living at the beginning of a profound shift of economic power away from the early industrial and post industrial economies of Europe and the USA, towards the emerging super-powers of India and China. The populations of these vast nations already share the western dream of hyper-mobility, to replace their lifestyles based around healthy bicycles, rickshaws and long walks with the speed and sedentary comfort of a car. The car-usage revolution is rapidly spreading east. And it will require huge amounts of cheap energy to achieve this.

There is constant debate about that most volatile of commodities – oil. Many independent experts have suggested that "Peak Oil" will occur within the next decade if indeed it has not already occurred as some claim. "Peak Oil" simply means the point when production of oil in the world has peaked in the quantity that can be extracted, refined and distributed cheaply and easily, before demand begins to exceed supply. When that happens, if even by a small margin, the cheap energy era will come, dramatically, to an end. The impact on standards of living in the western world will be enormous, and will not be without considerable social unrest which will also create its own significant economic consequences.

Optimistic scenarios are that before then new cheap sources of energy for transport will be discovered – hydrogen fuel cells, bio fuels (though this creates its own problems), farming of algae or perhaps unlimited cheap nuclear-generated electricity which can also be used to power cars. But such new technologies, which may take decades to put into place, will only be developed at a time when oil prices make such alternatives more economic. They are unlikely, at least in the short to medium term, to provide energy anything like as cheaply and easily as oil currently does.

There are other social-demographic and economic time bombs ticking in the background which may change patterns of living and travel choice. People are living longer, but larger numbers of retirees will no longer have the generous pension cover of the previous generation – income which made it possible for older people to continue to run a car well into retirement. Young people are now leaving university or college with substantial personal debt, and with graduate unemployment currently high, they can no longer take a driving test or purchase or insure that elusive first car.

If these scenarios continue to develop, they will in effect make many people in Britain – especially the younger, older and those on lower incomes – much poorer in terms of their purchasing power. Car ownership, far from heading towards stratospheric levels of near universal provision, will level out and could soon even decline. People will have no choice but to walk more.

As a society we should start to prepare for such a post-car age, not perceiving it as a disaster, but in terms of health, environment and quality of life, as an opportunity. Most people will not willingly give up the apparent freedom their car offers. However it is important to plan for a situation where an increasing number of people will be forced to do so, and will need to be given maximum support, incentive and encouragement to choose car-free, healthier lifestyles, in which walking not driving becomes the central focus of life. Everything that can be done should be done in terms of encouraging people to adopt car-free lifestyles, and this must mean cutting bus and train fares to a point where using the car is no longer, for individuals and families, the cheapest option. Far more safe options for walking and cycling need to be created.

This is already standard practice in countries such

as Germany, Austria, Switzerland, Italy, Spain, France and the Netherlands, but Britain is far behind in its thinking.

On a national level, this means land-use planning which sees the pedestrian in both urban and rural environments not as a "vulnerable road user" to be kept away from traffic behind barriers or in tunnels, but as someone to be encouraged for choosing an efficient and environmentally friendly mode of travel. Walkers are the most socially responsible citizens. Provisions for walkers should be central in the provision of all movement in the design and layout of both city centres and suburbs. Traffic is pollution and needs to be discouraged by both structural and fiscal measures. Investment should be switched away from road and car park building towards the creation of safe and attractive traffic-free routes for walkers, and cyclists, developing new pedestrian and cycling infrastructure in both town and countryside.

Central to this process of shifting focus away from speed towards quality of life is the idea of "Time Pollution". This is a concept developed by the environmentalist Professor John Whitelegg to indicate how faster journeys simply encourage people to lose those very time savings by travelling ever longer distances. For example faster roads, cars or railways generally result in people commuting longer distances to work or for leisure – what Whitelegg describes as a parallel "Space Pollution". Local public transport is important in reversing such trends because by its nature it supports and encourages walking in both town and countryside. The walk to the bus stop or railway station is a vital part of what is now called by many environmentalists "active travelling". Good, frequent local train and bus services supplement, support and extend the range of the walker to form part of a flexible, green network which can give environmentally sustainable access to a city or through the countryside.

Far from being a poor relation to car travel, the quality of experience is higher in terms of reduced stress and the exercise benefits of active travel, rather than literally being belted into a seat of a car as driver or passenger. Rural buses, for example can offer a superb way of discovering the countryside, small towns and villages, and of intermingling with rural communities that no car trip, however much faster, can ever match. And they can offer choice and flexibility to the walker for a variety of linear or point-to-point walks that the car, which restricts the user to circular walks, can never equal.

To work well, core bus and train services also need to be available at off-peak times such as evenings and Sundays so that people can access weekend and evening services and facilities such as theatres, pubs, clubs or cinemas without needing a car. This is especially relevant in rural areas where demand-responsive buses and shared taxis can and should allow people, especially young people living in rural communities, access to leisure facilities without a car, for example to theatres, cinemas and even night clubs in nearby towns. If the provision of such good networks results in individual decisions to delay or postpone car purchase, this is a net financial, environmental and personal health gain.

The American writer David Owen points out that in terms of environmental impacts per head of population, it is the city dweller not the country dweller, who makes least impact on the wider environment:

Most Americans, including most New Yorkers, think of New York City as an ecological nightmare, a wasteland of concrete and garbage and diesel fumes and traffic jams, but in comparison with the rest of America it's a model of environmental responsibility. In fact, by the most significant measures, New York is the greenest community in the United States. The average Manhattanite consumes gasoline at a rate that the country as a whole hasn't matched since the mid-1920s, when the most widely owned car in the United States was the Ford Model T. Eighty-two percent of employed Manhattan residents travel to work by public transit, by bicycle, or on foot. That's ten times the rate for Americans in general, and eight times the rate for workers in Los Angeles County.

New Yorkers as a whole generate 30% less greenhouse gases than the average USA citizen. As

Life without cars – on the island of Wangerooge, German Friesian Islands. Except for emergency vehicles, there are no cars. The island is served by a narrow gauge railway and pedestrians and cyclists are king. Luggage and shopping is carried in small wooden trolleys.

Sir Martin Doughty (1949-2009). Son of a former Derbyshire railwayman who took part in the Kinder Mass Trespass, Sir Martin was a keen walker. Former leader of Derbyshire County Council, chairman of the Peak District National Park Authority and the first chairman of Natural England, he was a passionate advocate of National Parks. He also supported networks of high-quality public transport to allow everyone, including people of limited means, to access the countryside. (Natural England)

The Mosaic Partnership is an initiative by the Campaign for National Parks to encourage individuals and groups from ethnic minority backgrounds to visit National Parks. This Mosaic group is enjoying a visit to a Dartmoor Tor. (CNP)

A typical Mosaic group of Asian ladies walking in New Forest National Park. (CNP)

Owen points out, as a measure per square foot New York's emissions are among the highest in the world. But the more meaningful measure is per household and per capita in which New Yorkers, living in high, energy efficient apartment blocks, actually generate 30% less greenhouse gases than the average American living in a leafy suburb, and much less than rural dwellers on an isolated ranch.

In this respect, 21st century Manhattan is a bit like the medieval city – high-density dwellings with key services centres within walking distance. But then the same can be said of a number of British cities which have kept at least something of their medieval, Georgian and even Victorian heart. People can and do live in cities such as York, Cambridge, Edinburgh, Durham, Oxford and above all London and get around on foot and by bike or by bus and underground. Modern Metro systems such as Nottingham's tram, Newcastle's Metro, Manchester's Metrolink and Sheffield's Supertram enable and encourage car-free lifestyles which include much more walking. According to a 2010 study by Campaign for Better Transport, Nottingham is now Britain's least car-dependent city.

But how do we get that vast percentage of Car Reliant and Car Dependent people out of their cars and onto their feet? To some extent it's like the old joke where a farmer, being asked the way by a couple of young hikers, replies: "If you take my advice, you wouldn't start out from here". Once you have decided to live somewhere or take a job where a car is essential to reach that job, then you are locked into car ownership. On the other hand if you choose to live in a city, town or even village when all the facilities – shops, pubs, doctor's surgery, library – are within walking or cycling distance, then car-free living is a real option. If you are able to live within walking distance of a railway station with a decent train service, or close enough to a good bus route, then lack of a car is not a big problem.

Sadly, one of the most pernicious effects of the present era of high car-based mobility is the loss and closure of rural and even suburban facilities in favour of centralised locations. This may save costs to the provider but only by passing travel costs on to the consumer. Closure of local shops and pubs, replaced by hypermarkets and leisure centres on ring roads outside towns, not only penalise the non-car owner, but constantly reinforces the car culture.

Most environmentally damaging of all is school choice which has resulted in millions of school children being carried across towns and cities in buses and cars, costing the nation billions in terms of hugely wasteful morning and late afternoon congestion of urban roads, plus additional traffic emissions, and, most critically, denying many children the opportunity for a health-giving walk or cycle ride to their neighbourhood school.

But by choosing to live and work somewhere where there are good local facilities, good public transport and above all good walking opportunities in the sense of local green space and well maintained footpath networks, life without a car is a natural choice. Walkers are Welcome towns are therefore natural candidates for a car-free lifestyle.

The easiest person to persuade to adopt a car-free lifestyle is someone who has not yet bought into the car culture, the young professional starting out on a career, probably a city dweller, who not having ever owned a car has learned as a teenager to get around on foot and to use the local bus and train networks.

It is economic pressures and market forces rather than idealism that are most likely to bring about behavioural changes in the decades ahead, as the cost of car ownership and usage rises. This could help to reverse the trend of rural migration into the countryside, if, as transport costs rise, city living, with access to facilities on foot or by frequent, cheap public transport becomes more economically attractive.

Consumerism – a lifestyle choice based on continuing acquisition of consumer goods, the latest technological gimmickry and "designer" clothing and accessories – is also likely to lose much of its appeal if there is a decline in disposable incomes. Likewise the process of computer-led alienation from a real to a virtual world of cyber technology – from computer games to electronic social networking as a substitute for real social contact – could begin to decline. Is it time for a rebellion against the e-technology age, reflecting the rebellion against the first Industrial Revolution two centuries ago?

Walking is perhaps one profoundly important way to rebel, like Ray Bradbury's Leonard Mead discovered, against the artificiality and constant manipulations of cyber-society. Walking is protest. Walking is about coming back to reality.

This is where we return to the insights of the great Romantic and post-Romantic poets, painters and naturalists. Just as the writers walked through the mountains or across moorland to discover something about their inner selves during the first Industrial Revolution, so there is a need for people in the 21st century to rediscover and re-create our relationship with the natural world, with the very wilderness and open spaces which are now threatened, worldwide, by the excesses of consumerism. Maybe it is the eco-warriors and climate change protesters who are the cutting edge of the movement to redefine man's relationship with the ecological systems on which we depend for our very physical existence and mental well-being. But maybe it is also walkers who can best rediscover the spiritual values arising from a deep and lasting respect for the natural environment.

Perhaps the darkest prophet of our time is the scientist and philosopher James Lovelock, who in the 1970s first formulated the concept of Gaia. The Gaia theory – named after Gaia the ancient Greek goddess of the Earth – postulates the Earth as a highly complex, living organism. This organism is in the process of reacting to the abuses of the planet by humankind with cataclysmic changes, including global warming which could eliminate human civilisation on the planet as we now know it. Whether Gaia theory is correct, or even if only partly so, man's relationship with the planet, and how we learn to live within the limits of the Earth's resources, are perhaps the greatest challenge facing humanity.

One way or another, society will have to change, either because it is forced to do so extremely painfully by the massive impact of catastrophic world climate-change related events and their aftermath, or by pre-emptive, planned measures to mitigate and reduce the impact of these events, and adaptation to the impacts that we can no longer prevent. There are precious few years left for mankind to exercise that choice.

Personal motorised transport, with its huge land-take and energy requirements, cannot be immune from these coming changes, however much we love our cars. But the more we can encourage people to walk and cycle, the greater their ability to cope, physically and mentally, with whatever major lifestyle adjustments lie ahead. The health benefits of regular walking will, by themselves, give people greater mental and physical strength to enable them better to adapt to whatever changes to our lifestyles that the future will present to us.

Persuading people to walk for their own health and well-being, and for the future of the planet, will require a multitude of educational mechanisms. It can be achieved through a variety of public information and education activity – books, magazines, newspapers, pamphlets, websites, broadcasts, films, talks, dvds, plays, interpretative displays. Much can and will be achieved through environmental education in its widest sense, in universities, schools, colleges, clubs, youth hostels, on guided and self guided walks. It is about encouraging people to experience and share the beauty and vulnerability of the countryside and wildlife habitats threatened by urban development, over-consumption, acidification of the oceans, rising population pressures and climate change.

But it will also require physical measures – creating new access opportunities in both urban and rural countryside to reduce car dependency and encourage green activities. It is why we need and must continue to protect and conserve our great National Parks, Areas of Outstanding Natural Beauty, Nature Reserves and historic National Trust estates and urban parks. It is why we also so urgently need better local and long distance footpath networks, accessible areas of open countryside, forest, shore, mountain, heath or moorland, as well as our more local countryside, areas where people can wander freely to re-connect themselves with the natural world. Walking a footpath is a way of returning to our roots in every sense. Walking is the supreme way of achieving that direct physical contact with the natural world, utilising all the senses, re-establishing our sense of what it is to be human.

Government agencies, such as Natural England, the Countryside Council for Wales and Scottish Natural Heritage, all have a major role in this process of education and provision as do National Park Authorities and Local Authorities. But critically important, as it has been over the past century and a half, is the voluntary sector. The great amenity organisations such as the National Trust, the Open Spaces Society, CPRE and CPRW, The Ramblers, YHA, the Campaign for National Parks, National Park societies, the Wildlife Trusts, all emerged from a post-Romantic awareness of the aesthetic and complex moral insights which come out of an understanding and appreciation of our finest areas of countryside. They have a continuing, vital role to campaign, to prompt, to urge, targeting not only their own membership, but the wider public and ultimately the local, national and international agencies of Government that have a crucial role both to provide for and to educate future generations in their stewardship of the planet.

What is certain is that walking, the most natural outdoor activity imaginable, will be central to that process.

Walk!

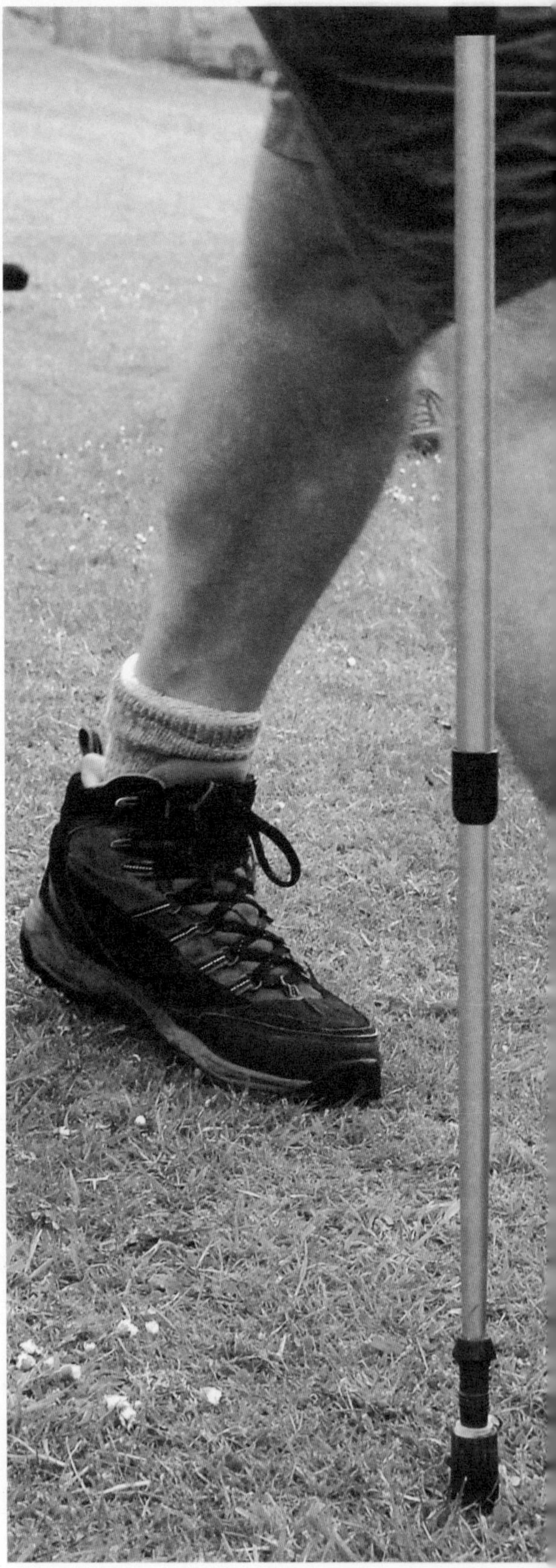

(Photos on pages 152-153 and 154-155: Yorkshire Post Newspapers)

Acknowledgements

All authors are magpies, this one more than most. Especially important sources for me have been Morris Marple's classic *Shank's Pony*, Sussman and Good's *Magic of Walking*, Tom Stephenson's *Forbidden Land*, Graham Murphy's *Founders of the National Trust*, John Cousin's excellent F*riends of the Lake District the Early Years*, and Ann Holt's invaluable *Origins and Early Years of the Ramblers' Association* and the Ramblers 50th anniversary collection of essays *Making Tracks*. Also important have been *Walk Magazine* and its predecessor *Rucksack* with articles going back many years, and, of course, the Ramblers' excellent website, a major source of factual information about walking, as are the magazines and websites of both the Open Spaces Society and the Campaign for Better Transport.

My gratitude also to Paul Salveson for his fascinating case study of Winter Hill in *Will Yo' No Come out o' Sunday Morning*, to Ian Brodie for sharing ideas and a very useful essay, to John Sparshatt and the Long Distance Walkers' Association for help with Chapter 5, and to Anne Beach and Steve Roberts of Natural England, Sheena Craig of Campaign for Better Transport, Peter Goldsmith of Harrogate Ramblers and the *Yorkshire Post* for helping to source and giving permission to use some iconic photographs.

But very especial thanks to Alan Mattingly, former Director of the Ramblers and Chair of the Campaign for National Parks, and to Ray Woolmore of Natural England, for reading the manuscript and being so generous with their comments (and any mistakes in the text are totally my own); the Campaign for National Parks and to Liz Wall of CNP who has done so much to make the book possible; to Ben and Chris for their wonderful forewords; and to my editor David Joy and publishers Great Northern without whom there would have been no book. And finally, and perhaps most of all, to Fleur, among many other things my constant walking companion and inspiration, without whom this book would most certainly not have been written.

Key Voluntary Organisations campaigning to conserve and access the British Countryside

Campaign for National Parks
6-7 Barnard Mews, London SW11 1QU
Tel 020 7924 4077
www.cnp.org.uk

The Ramblers
2nd Floor, Camelford House, 87-90 Albert Embankment, London SE1 7TW
Tel 020 7339 8500
www.ramblers.org.uk

The National Trust
PO Box 39, Warrington WA5 7WD
Tel 0844 800 1895
www.nationaltrust.org.uk

The Open Spaces Society
25 A Bell Street, Henley-on-Thames, Oxon RG9 2BA
Tel (01491) 573535
www.oss.org.uk

Scottish Rights of Way and Access Society
24 Annandale Street, Edinburgh, EH7 4AN
Tel 0131 558 1222
www.scotways.com

Youth Hostels Association
Trevelyan House, Dimple Road,
Matlock, Derbyshire DE4 3YH
Tel 01629 592600
www.yha.org.uk

Campaign to Protect Rural England
CPRE National Office, 128 Southwark Street, London, SE1 0SW
Tel 020 7981 2800
www.cpre.org.uk

Campaign for the Protection of Rural Wales
Ty Gwyn, 31 High Street, Welshpool, Powys SY21 7YD
Tel: 01938 552525 or 01938 556212
www.cprw.co.uk

Campaign for Better Transport
16 Waterside, 44-48 Wharf Road, London N1 7UX
Tel: 020 7566 6480
www.campaignforbettertransport.org.uk

John Muir Trust
41 Commercial Street, Edinburgh EH6 6JD
Tel: 0131 554 0114
www.jmt.org

Long Distance Walkers' Association
Bellevue, Princes Street, Ulverston, Cumbria LA12 7NB
www.ldwa.org

Select Bibliography

Allen, David Ellitson *The Naturalist in Britain – A Social History* (Allen Lane 1976)

Bird, William *Natural Thinking – Investigating the links between the Natural Environment, Biodiversity and Mental Health* (RSPB 2007)

Borrow, George *Wild Wales* (1862)

Bradbury, Ray *Twice 22 in Golden Apples of the Sun* (Avon 1953)

Brodie, Ian *The Origins of Rambling as a Form of Recreation* (unpublished manuscript 2009)

Brontë, Emily *Wuthering Heights* (1848; second edition with Charlotte Brontë's Introduction 1859)

Buchanan, Colin *Traffic in Towns* (HMSO 1963)

Christie, M & Matthews, J *The Economic and Social Value of Walking in England* (Ramblers' Association 2003)

Clare, John *Selected Poems* ed. Arthur Symons (Henry Frowe, 1908)

Cousins, John *Friends of the Lake District – the Early Years* (Centre for North West Regional Studies, Lancaster University 2009)

Darley, Gillian *Octavia Hill – Social Reformer and Founder of the National Trust* (Constable 1990)

De Quincy, Thomas *Confessions of an Opium Eater* (1821)

Dower, John *National Parks in England and Wales* (Cmnd. 6628, Ministry of Town and Country Planning, HMSO 1945)

Emerson, R W *Concord Walks* (Complete Works V12 1904)

Engels, Friedrich *Condition of the Working Class in England* (1844)

Fergusson, M; David, A; Skinner, I *Delivering Changes in Travel Behaviour – Lessons from Health Promotion* (IEEP 1999)

Gaskell, Elizabeth *Mary Barton* (1848)

Gaskell, Elizabeth *The Life of Charlotte Brontë* (1857)

Gissing, George *The Odd Women* (1873)

Gissing, George *The Private Papers of Henry Ryecroft* (Constable 1903)

Hardy, Thomas *Return of the Native* (1878)

Hardy, Thomas *Collected Poems* (Macmillan, 4th edition 1930)

Hazlitt, William *On Going on a Journey* (first published in *Table-Talk* 1822)

Hazlitt, William *First Acquaintance with the Poets* (first published in the *Liberal*, No 3 1823)

Heine, Heinrich *Harzreise* (1823)

Hillaby, John *Journey Through Britain* (Constable 1968)

Hillman, M *A Continuous Pedestrian Network* (paper given at the Walk 21 Conference 1997)

Hillman, M & Fawcett T *How we can Save the Planet* (Penguin 2004)

Holt, Ann (editor) *Making Tracks – a Celebration of Fifty Years of the Ramblers' Association* (Ramblers' Association 1985)

Holt, Ann *The Origins and Early Years of the Ramblers' Association* (Ramblers' Association 1995)

Hughes, Ted *The Hawk in the Rain* (Faber 1957)

Joad, C E M *A Charter for Ramblers* (Hutchinson 1933)

Kay-Shuttleworth, James Phillips *The Moral and Physical Condition of the Working Classes Employed in the Cotton Manufacture in Manchester*, (1832)

Lawrence, P; Maple, L & Sparshatt, J (editors) *The UK Trailwalker's Handbook* (LDWA/Cicerone 2009)

Lovelock, James *The Vanishing Face of Gaia: A Final Warning* (Allen Lane 2009)

MacEwen, Ann & Malcolm *National Parks: Conservation or Cosmetics?* (George Allen & Unwin 1982)

Marples, Morris *Shanks' Pony* (Dent 1959)

Mattingly, Alan *Tackle Rambling* (Stanley Paul 1981)

Mitchell, R & Popham, F *Effect of Exposure to Natural Environment on Health Inequalities: an Observational Population Study* (*The Lancet* 2008;372:1655-660)

Moritz, Karl Philipp *Journeys of a German in England* (1782) (Translated by Reginald Nettel – Eland 1983)

Muir, John *The Forests of Yosemite Park* (*Atlantic Monthly* 1900 – quoted in Sussman & Goode)

Mumford, Lewis *The Highway and the City* (essay collection) (New York: Harcourt, Brace & World 1963)

Murphy, Graham *Founders of the National Trust* (National Trust – new edition 2002)

Nicholson, Norman *The Lakers – the First Tourists* (Robert Hale 1955)

Nicholson, Norman *Collected Poems* (Faber & Faber 1994)

Owen, David *Green Manhattan – Why New York is the Greenest City in the U.S.* (in *The New Yorker* magazine 18 October 2004)

Paine, Thomas *The Rights of Man* (1791)

Phillips, John *Excursions in Yorkshire by the North Eastern Railway* (1853)

Phillips, Bevan G *Tourists' Guide to the East and North Ridings of Yorkshire* (4th Edition – Stanford 1887)

Porter, Roy *English Society in the Eighteenth Century* (Pelican 1982)

Priestley, J B *English Journey* (1934 – 75th anniversary edition, Great Northern Books 2009)

Riddall, John & Trevelyan, John *Rights of Way – A Guide to Law and Practice* (3rd edition – Open Spaces Society and Ramblers' Association 2001)

Royal Commission on Environmental Pollution 18th Report on Transport on the Environment (HMSO 1994), *20th Report Developments since 1994* (Stationery Office 1997)

Ruskin, John *Modern Painters II* (1846)

Salveson, Paul *Will Yo' Come O Sunday Morning?* (Red Rose Publishing 1982)

Sharp, David (editor) *Ramblers' Ways* (David & Charles 1980)

Shelley, P B *A Defence of Poetry* (1821)

Shoard, Marion *This Land is our Land* (Paladin 1987)

Shoard, Marion *A Right to Roam* (Oxford 1999)

Smith, Roly (editor) *Kinder Scout – Portrait of a Mountain* (Derbyshire County Council 2002)

Solnit, Rebecca *Wanderlust – A History of Walking* (Verso 2001)

Speakman, Colin *Adam Sedgwick, Geologist and Dalesman* (Broadoak Press/Trinity College Cambridge 1982)

Speakman, Fleur & Speakman, Colin *Walking in the Black Forest* (Cicerone 1990)

Statham, Derek *An Eye to Perceive – Memories of a National Park Officer* (North York Moors Association 2010)

Stephenson, Tom *The Pennine Way* (HM Stationery Office 1980)

Stephenson, Tom *Forbidden Land – the Struggle for Access to Mountain and Moorland* (edited Ann Holt) (Manchester University Press 1989)

Stevenson, Robert Louis *Travels with a Donkey in the Cevennes* (1862)

Sussman, Aaron & Goode, Ruth *The Magic of Walking* (Simon & Schuster 1980)

Symonds, H H *Walking in the Lake District* (Chambers 1933)

Thomas, Edward *Oxford* (A & C Black 1903)

Thomas, Edward *The Poems of Edward Thomas* (ed R. George Thomas) (Oxford University Press, 1978)

Thoreau, Henry David *Walden* (1854)

Thoreau, Henry David *Excursions* (1863)

Trevelyan, George *Walking – Essay in Clio, A Muse and Other Essays* (Longmans, Green & Co 1913)

Wainwright W A *Pennine Way Companion* (Westmorland Gazette 1968)

Wainwright W A *A Coast to Coast Walk* (Westmorland Gazette 1973)

Whitelegg, John *Transport for a Sustainable Future: The Case for Europe* (Belhaven Press, 1993)

Wordsworth, Dorothy *Grasmere Journal* (1802)

Wordsworth, William *The Prelude* (1805)

Wordsworth, William *Complete Poems* (1850)

Wordsworth, William *A Complete Guide to the Lakes* (Fourth Edition 1853)

Wyatt, John *The Gentle Art of Country Walking* (Random House 1993)

Index